CHRISTMAS 1993.

DARLING,
　　LETS EAT MALAY 1994!!

　　ALL MY LOVE & HAVE
　A LOVELY CHRISTMAS

　　　　HARRY.

MORE
CAPE MALAY
COOKING

FALDELA WILLIAMS

Photography by Juan Espi
Illustrations by Marianne Saddington

STRUIK TIMMINS

Struik Timmins
(a member of The Struik Publishing Group (Pty) Ltd)
Cornelis Struik House
80 McKenzie Street
Cape Town 8001

Reg. No.: 71/09721/07

First published 1991
Second impression 1992

Text © Faldela Williams 1991, 1992
Photographs and illustrations © The Struik Publishing Group (Pty) Ltd. 1991, 1992

All rights reserved. No part of this publication may be reproduced, stored in a retrieval system, or transmitted, in any form or by any means, electronic, mechanical, photocopying, recording or otherwise without the prior written permission of the copyright owners.

Editor: Inge du Plessis
Designer: Janice Evans
Assistant designer: Lellyn Creamer
Cover designer: Abdul Amien
Layout artist: Clarence Clark
Photographer: Juan Espi
Stylist: Marine Williams
Illustrator: Marianne Saddington

Typesetting by BellSet, Cape Town
Reproduction by Unifoto (Pty) Ltd, Cape Town
Printed and bound by Leefung-Asco Printers Ltd, Hong Kong

ISBN 0 86978 538 9

ACKNOWLEDGEMENTS

Algamdulillah! My most gracious thanks to our Creator.

I would also like to extend my heartfelt thanks to my parents, family, friends, neighbours, in fact, our entire community for their wonderful support.

Special thanks must be given to my friends who helped with some of the recipes: Shaheeda Firfirey, Shaheeda Ebrahim, Nabeweya Kamaldien, Zainab Saliem and Jorayda Moos.

To my neighbours and friends for the use of their delicate chinaware, ornate brassware and beautiful scarves, and especially to Nabeweya Kamaldien, Shehaam Dollie, Farieda Dollie, Faeza Dollie, Fahimoenisa Moosa, Aunty Gawa Amos, Aunty Jay, Rabiyah Ally, Mureeda Samaai, Aunty Laygie Basadien, Tougeeda Basadien, Galiedja Martin and my sister, Fawzia van der Westhuizen. Thanks also to Dudley Fillies for the spice box.

To Ebrahim Shukran for his wonderful support and my children, Riefqah, Saadiq and Aisha, may your patience be rewarded!

In conclusion we ask The Almighty to accept this endeavour and to make it a success. Inshallah!

CONTENTS

Metric Conversion 4
Introduction 5
Spices, Herbs and Seasonings 7
Snacks 11
Seafood 19
Chicken 27
Meat 32
Vegetables, Sambals and Atjars 40
Breads and Pizzas 47
Biscuits and Pastries 55
Cakes and Desserts 63
Beverages 76
Eid Celebration Dinner 79
Bride's Dinner Basket 82
Catering for Large Numbers 88
Outdoor Entertaining 92
Index 96

METRIC CONVERSION

Practical equivalents
OVEN TEMPERATURES

	°C	°F
Cool	140	275
	150	300
Moderate	160	325
	180	350
Moderately hot	190	375
	200	400
Hot	220	425
	230	450

METRIC VOLUME EQUIVALENTS

Measuring Cup	Tablespoon	Teaspoon
60 ml = ¼ cup	15 ml = 1T	1 ml = ¼t
80 ml = ⅓ cup	30 ml = 2T	2,5 ml = ½t
125 ml = ½ cup	45 ml = 3T	5 ml = 1t
200 ml = ¾ cup	60 ml = 4T	7,5 ml = 1½t
250 ml = 1 cup		10 ml = 2t
500 ml = 2 cups		15 ml = 3t
750 ml = 3 cups		20 ml = 4t
1 litre = 4 cups		

Approximate mass per 250 ml (1 cup)

Barley	200 g
Beans, dried	200 g
Breadcrumbs,	
fresh	70 g
dried	140 g
Butter	230 g
Cheese,	
cream or cottage	250 g
grated	100 g
Chickpeas	200 g
Cocoa powder	100 g
Coconut, desiccated	80 g
Dried fruit: raisins,	
currants, dates	150 g
Flour	
brown bread	120 g
cake	120 g
cornflour	120 g
wholewheat	130 g
Lentils	200 g
Nuts,	
chopped	100 g
whole	150 g
Oats, rolled	90 g
Peas, dried split	200 g
Rice	200 g
Sugar,	
castor	210 g
granulated	200 g
icing	130 g
Vegetables, frozen mixed	250 g
Wheat, crushed	200 g

INTRODUCTION

Cape Malay cooking – essentially a rich potpourri of tastes from the kitchens of East and West – has been influenced largely by Indonesian, Indian, Arabian, Turkish, Dutch and English cuisine.

From Java and the neighbouring Indonesian islands, the forefathers of the Cape Malay community reached the Cape as early as 1667 as slaves to the predominantly Dutch population then resident at the Cape. These Malay slaves brought with them the oriental spices that they used so masterfully and also introduced a variety of exotic dishes – from Indian samoosas, puris and rotis to Indonesian bobotok which, with a little adaptation, was transformed into the ever-popular bobotie of today. Owing to their extraordinary cooking skills, they were in constant demand in the Dutch households. In this way, they not only acquired the skills to prepare traditional Dutch fare, but soon adapted these dishes to suit the Malay palate by adding their own choice of exotic spices. It is for this reason that Cape Malay confectionery shows such a strong Western and particularly Dutch influence.

The Cape Malays adhere strictly to the Muslim religion and customs which, in turn, influence their culinary habits. Any food eaten by a Muslim should be *Halaal* or lawful. Pork, blood and alcohol are forbidden, as is any animal or bird that has not been slaughtered in a humane way. Furthermore, there is a multitude of religious festivals and ceremonies, when special foods are prepared and eaten. The principal fast in the Muslim religion is *Ramadan* – the ninth month of the Islamic calendar – during which no food may be eaten or water drunk after sunrise or before sunset. Before sunrise, a substantial breakfast is eaten. At sunset, throughout the month of Ramadan, it is customary to present neighbours with Ramadan gifts consisting of small plates laden with slices of cake and biscuits to be enjoyed at nightfall. (Frequent mention has been made in the confectionery sections of bakes suitable for these gifts.) This is followed by a substantial dinner comprising soup or *boeber* (a thick, milky drink) and, as a main meal, bredie or whatever is fancied. Then comes the picturesque *Festival of Charity* (Eidul-fitr), celebrated at the conclusion of Ramadan, during which Malay cooks spend many hours preparing special dishes to be shared with the poor. An entire chapter has been set aside for the Eid celebration dinner, with such dishes as Crayfish curry (page 21), Mutton breyani (page 80), Pot-roast leg of lamb (page 79), Fruit trifle (page 81) and Tropical fruit punch (page 77). The *Feast of Sacrifice* (Eidul-Adha) is usually celebrated about 70 days after Ramadan, when a young lamb or goat is sacrificed and a third of the meat is shared with family and friends.

A Malay funeral is a community affair, when family, friends and neighbours gather to mourn the dead. It is preceded by rituals lasting from the day of death to several days after the burial. At the end of the burial, mourners gather at the home of the deceased, where a meal is served. This is usually a dish such as Wortel en Ertjie Bredie (page 91), Sugar bean bredie (page 88) or Mutton curry (page 89). (This is where the chapter dealing with catering for large numbers comes in very handy.) Another ceremony in the Cape Malay custom which is prescriptive to some degree regarding culinary habits, is the *doop* (naming of the baby), which usually takes place a week after birth. At the ceremony a lock of hair is cut from the baby's head and something sweet, such as a date, sugar or honey is placed on the baby's lips while prayers are held. At the conclusion of this ceremony, family and guests settle down to tea and *melktert*. The serving of melktert at a *doopmaal* (meal served after the doop) has become such an established tradition that it is almost synonymous with the ceremony that precedes it. Recently, however, Custard tartlets (page 74) have also become acceptable fare at a doopmaal.

Malay weddings are festive, colourful and very elaborate ceremonies, usually with two separate receptions – one for the bridegroom and one for the bride. The receptions could either take the form of a substantial lunch or dinner, or it could be a tea, where cakes and sweets are served. Traditionally, the bridegroom presents the bride with a *bride's dinner basket* – carefully prepared traditional foods wrapped in cellophane and decorated with pretty bows and flowers. An entire chapter has been set aside for the preparation of the bride's dinner basket and mention has been made throughout the book of dishes suitable for a wedding reception dinner.

In the chapters dealing with breads, biscuits and cakes, frequent mention is made of *barakats* – these are simply gifts presented at special occasions. The engagement *barakat*, for example, is presented by the bride-to-be to her future husband's relatives and consists of fancy cakes and biscuits wrapped in cellophane. The *ghajad barakat* is presented at special prayer evenings which are usually held on Thursday or Sunday nights.

Finally, it is important to point out that this book deals not only with traditional Cape Malay cooking, but also with modern recipes and recipes of Western origin which have been adopted by the Cape Malays. There are a multitude of reasons for this, the most important being that many of the Western bakes have become so popular in Cape Malay homes that they are included in engagement and ghajad barakats, presented to neighbours at Ramadan and eaten at special occasions such as weddings and the doopmaal. It is evident, therefore, that many bakes and foods, although not of Malay origin, have in their own way become part of the culinary tradition of the Cape Malays.

This book is dedicated to the young and old who enjoy savouring spicy food.

Bis'millah!

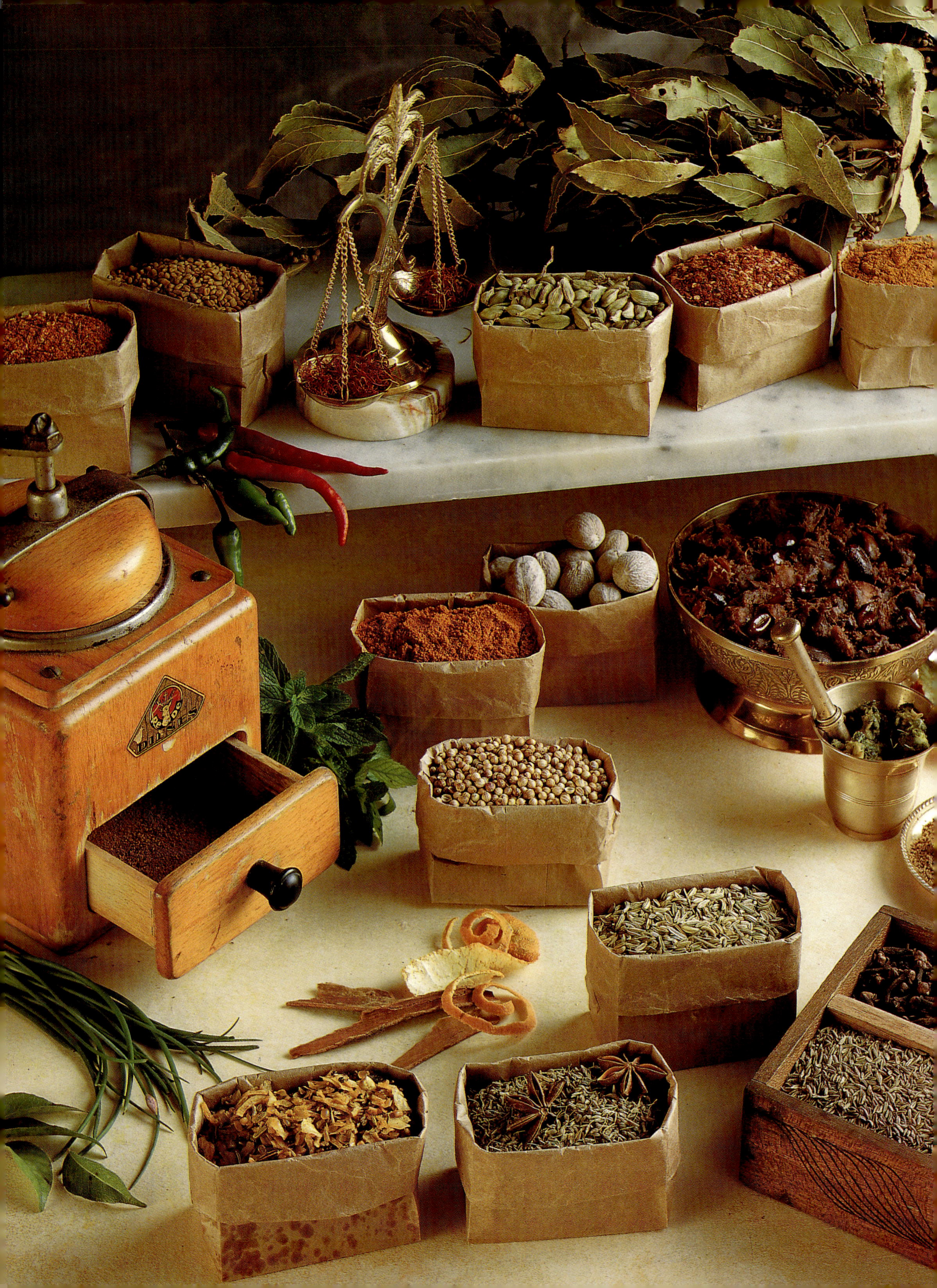

Spices, Herbs and Seasonings

On their arrival at the Cape over 300 years ago, Malay cooks brought with them a diverse culinary tradition characterized by the art of seasoning. The use of aromatic spices, herbs and seasonings even today forms the heart of Malay cooking, and flavours range from the pungency of hot chillies to the fragrance of nutmeg, cinnamon and cloves. A knowledge of the different flavours and aromas imparted by these ingredients, as well as their shelf life and method of preparation, is important when preparing food. All spices, especially ground spices, diminish in flavour with time, so use fresh, whole spices and grind them as you need them. Buy your spices from a recognized spice shop and store in airtight containers in a cool, dry place as they tend to lose their freshness if exposed for too long to air, heat and moisture.

Allspice
This sun-dried berry of the West Indian pimento tree seems to combine the flavours of nutmeg, cinnamon and cloves, hence its name. It is used in the preparation of many masalas and is therefore a popular spice for flavouring curries, soups and bredies. Ground allspice can also be used in desserts, cakes and biscuits.

Aniseed
The seeds of the anise plant – similar in shape to that of jeera and barishap – is used mainly in confectionery because of its warm, sweet, liquorice flavour. Aniseed should be used sparingly, as the flavour can be overpowering. Star aniseed, so called because of its star shape, is rarely used on its own but is ground and used in breyani masala and garam masala.

Barishap
Also known as fennel, barishap is a strong-smelling yellow-flowered plant, whose seeds look very much like jeera but are fatter and less elongated. These aromatic seeds have a warm, slightly bitter, aniseed flavour and are used in fish dishes and savoury dishes such as *chevra* (a mixture of cornflakes, popped rice, nuts, spices and braised onions). Ground barishap is very often used in breyani masala, and is ideal to chew after a spicy meal, as it freshens the breath.

Bay leaf
The bay leaf comes from the sweet bay or true laurel tree. It is aromatic with a slightly bitter taste and is used in the preparation of dishes such as pickled fish, sosaties and denningvleis. Use sparingly and always discard the leaves before serving. For a more delicate flavour, some cooks prefer to use lemon leaves.

Borrie
Borrie, also called turmeric, is a deep yellow, ground spice obtained from the dried root of a plant related to ginger. It has a slightly bitter taste and care should be taken not to exceed the amount recommended in a recipe. Borrie is used mainly for flavouring curries, pickled fish and sosaties and for colouring yellow rice.

Cardamom
Known as elachi in the Indian community, dried cardamom seed pods are available in two varieties – green and white. It is best to buy cardamom seeds in small quantities and to use as needed, since they quickly lose their pungent aroma and distinctive flavour after they have been ground. The aromatic dark-brown seeds are generally left whole, but are lightly crushed for curries, breyanis and rice dishes. Ground cardamom is also used in the preparation of puddings, koesisters, biscuits and cakes.

Chilli
There are 30 different varieties of chilli, some much sharper than others. Unripe or green chillies are juicier, with more flavour, while ripe or red chillies are hotter. Pounded or liquidized chillies mixed with a little oil and salt can be stored in sealed containers in a refrigerator. Prepare dried chillies for cooking by tearing them into pieces and soaking them in hot water for 10 minutes to soften. Chillies, fresh or dried, are important ingredients in most curry dishes, chutneys and sambals.

Chilli powder
Generally red in colour and made from dried red chillies, chilli powder imparts to food the distinctive bite which is characteristic of Malay dishes. It is also excellent for foods which need a bit of colour. Chilli powder can be used on chops and fish as a substitute for freshly ground black pepper.

Chives
This small, purple-flowered plant has long slender hollow leaves which are excellent for garnishing salads and savoury dishes such as seafoods. It is also a more subtle substitute for the stronger flavoured onion.

Cinnamon
Cinnamon is the spice obtained from the yellowish-brown bark of a tropical tree and has a rich, spicy aroma and a delicious, sweet flavour. In Malay cooking, stick cinnamon is added to curries, breyanis, vegetables, puddings and desserts. Ground cinnamon is also used in melktert and other confectionery.

Cloves
Cloves are the dried, unopened flower buds of yet another tree indigenous to Indonesia. They have a pronounced aroma and a strong, almost bitingly sharp, spicy taste. Cloves are used to flavour many savoury and sweet dishes, and the flavour blends well with other spices such as cinnamon, allspice and nutmeg. Ground cloves are stronger in flavour than whole ones, so use only a pinch, for the flavour can be overpowering.

Curry leaves
These are available fresh or dried. Fresh curry leaves are used mainly for garnishing curry dishes while dried ones are used in the preparation of leaf masalas and for adding extra flavour to savouries such as chevra.

Curry powder
Curry powder – a mixture of borrie, whole koljander, jeera, ginger, black peppercorns, chilli and mustard seeds – is at its best when all the spices are freshly ground or grated. Many commercial preparations, including curry paste, are available, but these do not have quite the flavour of fresh spices and tend to lend a sameness to everything in which they are used. Malay people mostly use masalas in cooking and only use curry powder in sweet-and-sour curry dishes such as penang curry, sosaties, bobotie and pickled fish.

Dhunia
This is the name given to fresh coriander leaves which are used for both garnishing and flavouring curry dishes or savouries such as samoosas. Pounded dhunia leaves are also an important ingredient for chutneys. When crushed, dhunia leaves have an unmistakably pungent smell. They can also be chopped and used as a substitute for parsley.

Garlic
A popular herb and a member of the onion family, garlic is often used fresh in combination with fresh root ginger. In the seasoning of fish dishes, however, only garlic is used. Garlic, if minced or liquidized with a little oil and salt, will last well in the refrigerator.

Ginger
Ginger, as with nearly all spices, contains a volatile oil that gives it its distinctive flavour which is aromatic, biting and slightly sweet. Fresh ginger is indispensable when making curries and breyanis and if mixed with garlic makes an excellent meat tenderizer. Dried whole ginger is more fibrous and pungent and less aromatic than fresh ginger. It can be powdered easily and retains its spicy flavour for a long time. Ground ginger is used in flavouring koesisters, konfyts, puddings and cakes.

Jeera
Jeera – the Malay and Indian word for cumin – is a caraway-shaped seed similar to that of barishap but slightly more bitter. When the seeds are ground, the powder has a distinctive green colour. Jeera is an important ingredient in masalas such as breyani and garam masala and is therefore always used in curries and breyanis.

Koljander
Also known as coriander, this is a seed which tastes sweet and aromatic and should be roasted before being ground in order to bring out its curry-like flavour. Koljander seeds crushed together with jeera are widely used in curries and other meat dishes.

Mace
Mace comes from the same tree as nutmeg and is made from the dried aril covering the nutmeg seed. Mace imparts a slightly bitter taste and is used in combination with other spices to make garam masala.

Masala
Masala is a fragrant blend of spices used in curries, breyanis, atjars and many other savoury dishes. There are many different varieties of wet and dry masala, such as special masala for fish (with mustard seeds), vegetables, atjars, chutneys, breyanis and rice dishes. Buy freshly ground masala from a spice shop or make your own by using the spices best suited to the particular dish you are preparing. You can grind your spices with a pestle and mortar, a blender or a food processor.

Atjar masala is a special mixture of spices such as mustard seed, chilli powder, borrie, ground methi and salt, and is specifically made for atjar, although it can also be used to garnish white rice. Oil is added to the mixture of spices to make a thick paste.

Breyani masala is made with whole jeera seeds, koljander, barishap, bay leaves, cardamom, cinnamon and star aniseed. Roast and grind before using in breyanis.

Garam masala is a mixture of cinnamon, cloves, jeera, cardamom, black pepper, nutmeg, mace and koljander and lends a fragrant, rather than hot, quality to food. Garam masala is sometimes combined with other spices and added to meat dishes at the frying stage or during the last few minutes of cooking. Alternatively, it can be sprinkled over the food just before it is served. It is also a perfect substitute for breyani masala.

Green masala contains pounded fresh ginger, garlic, green chilli and dhunia leaves and is used in savoury frikkadels, curries and salads.

Leaf masala, of which there are many varieties, include red leaf and yellow leaf masala which both contain chilli powder. The only difference between these two masalas is that yellow leaf masala is milder because it contains less curry powder than red leaf masala.

Methi
Methi, also known as fenugreek, has a hard, lentil-type seed which is ground with other spices to make curry powder or methi masala which is used to flavour some rice and vegetable dishes. This spice has an astringent aroma and should be used sparingly.

Mint
When chopped, this clean-tasting herb blends well with savoury fillings for samoosas. Mint is very easy to grow and no garden, no matter how small, need be without this most useful herb. Mint leaves are used to great advantage for garnishing fresh fruit salads and punch.

Mustard seed
The mustard seed is a dark reddish-brown seed, slightly larger than a poppy seed. Seafood dishes, atjars and pickles are greatly enhanced when flavoured with mustard seeds. Whole mustard seeds may be added to atjar masala for a more pungent flavour.

Naartjie peel
This is one of the cheapest and most rewarding flavouring agents for puddings, desserts and vegetables and it is a great pity that so few people take the trouble to experiment with it nowadays. The peel is left out to dry in the sun, then ground into a powder and stored in an airtight jar for later use. It blends well with cardamom and cinnamon.

Nutmeg
Nutmeg comes from the same tree as mace. The seed of the fruit is the nutmeg and the dried, reddish skin that covers the nutmeg is mace. Grated or ground nutmeg is frequently used as a garnish for boiled vegetables, and as a flavouring agent in bredies and confectionery.

Rose-water
A fragrant essence distilled from rose petals and traditionally used by Malay cooks to flavour *boeber* (a rich milky drink) and puddings. Nowadays rose-water is also used in the making of Turkish Delight and is an essential ingredient in rose syrup which is used to flavour milkshakes and falooda jelly. Apart from its uses in foods, rose-water, if diluted, can also be used as a skin freshener.

Saffron
Saffron is by far the rarest and most expensive spice in the world. The name is derived from the Arabic word *Za'faran* meaning yellow. The dark, reddish-orange stamens of the wild crocus are used mainly for colouring and flavouring rice dishes and puddings. It is one of the most wonderful spices to use in breyanis, boeber and savoury rice. First infuse the saffron in hot water or add directly to the meat marinade when making breyani.

Tamarind
This dark-brown fruit of a tropical tree tastes very much like an apricot and date mixture. Its sweet-and-sour flavour makes it an excellent ingredient in sosaties and denningvleis. Children love to suck on the fresh fruit.

Samoosas with, from right to left, Fish filling, Mince filling (back), Potato filling, Mixed vegetable filling and Chicken filling.

10 • MORE CAPE MALAY COOKING

Snacks

Snacks play an important role in Malay cuisine and are very versatile in the sense that they can be served as finger foods, light meals or as a preamble to a main meal, simply by adapting them slightly. As these snack recipes are fairly substantial in themselves, they are ideal for finger foods at informal gatherings and meetings. By combining a snack with a side dish such as a salad, it can be transformed into a light meal, especially popular with children. If, however, it is served as a starter, choose the recipe best suited to the main course and serve small portions so that your guests can enjoy the rest of the meal.

SAMOOSAS

*Although Indian in origin, samoosas are also a favourite snack of the Cape Malays. Leftover strips of pur can be deep-fried to make a crunchy snack called **paaper** and if crushed can be served over soup.*

PUR (PASTRY)
**750 ml cake flour
pinch of borrie (turmeric)
2,5 ml salt
250 ml cold water
5 ml white vinegar
75 ml cooking oil for spreading**

Preheat oven to 200 °C. Sift flour, borrie and salt into a mixing bowl. Combine water and vinegar and mix with flour to a fairly stiff mixture, the consistency of bread dough. Divide into 12 balls. Working with four balls of dough at a time, roll each into a round the size of a large saucer (15 cm in diameter). Using your fingers, spread a little oil on each round, covering it well so that it does not stick during cooking. Sprinkle lightly with flour and place one round on top of the other, oily sides together. You will now have two rounds, each made up of a double layer of dough. Oil and flour the tops in the same way as before. Sandwich these together to form a single pile of four rounds, each layer of which has been oiled and dusted with flour. Repeat with remaining balls of dough. Gently roll out piles of rounds on a lightly floured board to a 25 cm diameter circle or oval. Turn the pastry from time to time. Place the rolled out pastry on an ungreased baking sheet and bake for 2–3 minutes or until the pastry has puffed up slightly. Remove from oven, cut into strips 6 cm wide and 25–30 cm long, then separate into thin layers before the pastry cools down. Cover with a damp cloth to prevent the pastry from drying out.

To fold samoosas: Holding the strip of pastry in your left hand, pull the bottom corner across as indicated (Fig. 1). Fold upwards, adjusting edges to form a triangle with sharp corners and a pocket in which to place filling (Fig. 2). Fill with 10 ml filling, then continue folding the pastry across the top of the triangle to seal off the opening. Tuck edges round to form a neat triangle (Fig. 3). Seal off the small remaining edge with a paste of flour and water (Fig. 4). Lightly pinch two bottom edges together to puff it up before you fry it.

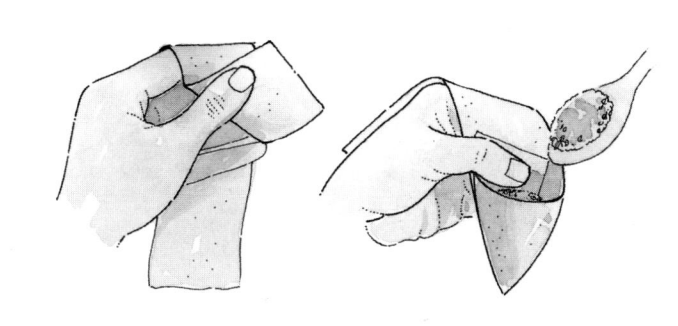

Fig. 1   **Fig. 2**

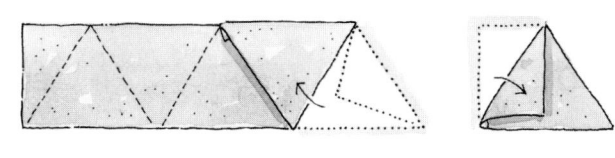

Fig. 3   **Fig. 4**

To cook samoosas: Deep-fry samoosas in hot oil over medium heat, turning once or twice to ensure that they are evenly cooked. When golden brown, remove from oil with a slotted spoon and drain on paper towel. Serve immediately.
MAKES 48.

Mince Filling

500 g steak or mutton mince
5 ml salt
5 ml ground jeera (cumin)
5 ml crushed, dried chillies or chilli powder
5 ml crushed garlic
5 ml grated fresh root ginger
2,5 ml borrie (turmeric)
½ bunch dhunia (coriander) leaves, chopped
2 onions, chopped
30 ml freshly chopped mint (optional)

Wash and drain mince. Braise in a heavy-based frying pan until all the liquid has evaporated, stirring to prevent sticking and lumps forming. Add salt, jeera, chillies or chilli powder, garlic, ginger, borrie and dhunia leaves. Add onions and braise until well blended and mixture is fairly dry. Add mint, if using, and mix well. Remove from heat and allow to cool before filling samoosas.
FILLS ABOUT 80 SAMOOSAS.

Cook's tip
Before using fresh root ginger in food, first peel the ginger, then grate it to a pulp.

Potato Filling

500 g potatoes, peeled and diced
15 ml cooking oil
15 ml butter
2,5 ml mustard seeds
1 medium onion, chopped
2,5 ml borrie (turmeric)
2,5 ml chilli powder
2,5 ml salt

Boil potatoes until soft. Heat oil and butter together and add mustard seeds. When seeds start popping, add onion and fry for about 5 minutes until golden brown. Add diced potatoes, borrie, chilli and salt and cook for 10 minutes, or until all the liquid has evaporated. Allow to cool before filling samoosas.
FILLS ABOUT 50 SAMOOSAS.

Fish Filling

500 g any firm fresh fish
2 onions, finely chopped
2 green chillies, finely chopped
5 ml salt
30 ml lemon juice
60 ml chopped dhunia (coriander) leaves

Boil fish until tender, then drain and flake. Add onions, chillies, salt, lemon juice and dhunia leaves while fish is still warm. Allow to cool before filling samoosas.
FILLS 30–36 SAMOOSAS.

Mixed Vegetable Filling

30 ml cooking oil
5 curry leaves
1 large onion, finely chopped
1 green chilli, finely chopped
5 ml crushed garlic
5 ml ground jeera (cumin)
2,5 ml borrie (turmeric)
salt to taste
500 ml frozen mixed vegetables
30 ml chopped dhunia (coriander) leaves
10 ml chopped chives

Heat oil, add curry leaves and after a few seconds add onion, chilli, garlic, jeera, borrie and salt. Allow to simmer for about 10 minutes. Add vegetables and cook a further 10 minutes. Mix in dhunia leaves and chopped chives when mixture has cooled.
FILLS ABOUT 36 SAMOOSAS.

Chicken Filling

500 g chicken breasts
10 ml crushed garlic
5 ml grated fresh root ginger
1 green chilli, finely chopped
2,5 ml borrie (turmeric)
10 ml garam masala
30 ml chopped dhunia (coriander) leaves
1 small onion, grated
salt to taste

Skin and fillet chicken breasts. Mix garlic, ginger and chilli together and rub into chicken fillets. Steam for about 15 minutes over medium heat, flake and combine with rest of ingredients. Allow to cool before filling samoosas.
FILLS ABOUT 36 SAMOOSAS.

SAVOURY PIES

A favourite snack for weddings, informal gatherings or buffet suppers, and can be varied with different fillings.

PUFF PASTRY
(Makes 2 kg dough)
8 x 250 ml cake flour
15 ml cream of tartar
250 ml cornflour
2 extra-large egg yolks
10 ml white vinegar
5 ml salt
10 ml sugar
200 g margarine
500 ml ice water
750 g cold butter

You need four mixing bowls for this recipe. Bowl 1: sift 250 ml cake flour and 10 ml cream of tartar and reserve for sprinkling. Bowl 2: sift 250 ml cornflour and 5 ml cream of tartar and reserve for sprinkling. Bowl 3: beat egg yolks and vinegar and set aside. Bowl 4: sift remaining flour with salt and sugar and rub in margarine until mixture resembles coarse breadcrumbs. Add ice water to egg and vinegar mixture. Add gradually to flour, working very lightly to form a soft, smooth and elastic dough. Sprinkle a little cornflour mixture over and, on a lightly floured surface, roll out the dough into a rectangle. Divide the 750 g butter into five equal portions. Grate one portion over two-thirds of dough and sprinkle a little cornflour mixture over. Fold a third of the dough over, sprinkling top with cornflour mixture, then fold over other third like an envelope. Set aside for at least 30 minutes. Repeat this process until all the butter has been used, sprinkling with reserved flour mixture. Wrap dough in waxed paper and refrigerate for 12 hours before use.

To make pies: Preheat oven to 220 °C. Roll out puff pastry on a floured surface to a thickness of 5 mm. Cut out pastry rounds 7,5 cm in diameter or 7,5 cm squares and place about 10 ml filling in centre of half of them. Place remaining pastry rounds or squares on top and seal edges. Brush with beaten egg, arrange on baking sheet and bake for 15 minutes. Lower temperature to 180 °C and bake a further 10 minutes or until pastry is golden brown. Serve hot.
MAKES ABOUT 75 PIES.

Cook's tip
When making pastry remember:
- *Keep your hands, utensils and ingredients as cold as possible while working with the dough so that the grated butter can remain in layers between the layers of dough.*
- *Roll out the dough lightly and evenly; but do not press it with rolling pin.*
- *Do not pull or stretch dough while rolling out.*
- *Do not handle dough too much.*
- *Dough can be tightly wrapped in clingwrap and frozen for up to three months.*

Curry Mince Filling

500 g steak or mutton mince
2 onions, chopped
15 ml cooking oil
10 ml crushed garlic
5 ml grated fresh root ginger
5 ml salt
5 ml borrie (turmeric)
10 ml roasted masala
5 ml garam masala

Wash mince and drain well. Sauté onions in heated oil until transparent, about 5 minutes. Add mince and cook for about 15 minutes over medium heat, stirring frequently. Add rest of ingredients and cook until all the liquid has evaporated, about 30 minutes. Allow to cool before filling pies.
FILLS 75 PIES.

Steak and Kidney Filling

500 g sirloin steak
1 ox or 6 lamb kidneys
2 onions, chopped
15 ml cooking oil
10 ml crushed garlic
5 ml salt
5 ml freshly ground black pepper
2,5 ml grated nutmeg
2,5 ml ground cloves
5 ml crushed, dried red chillies
100 ml sago, soaked in 125 ml water for 10 minutes
3 hard-boiled eggs, grated (optional)

Cube steak. Remove membrane from kidneys and cut into small cubes. Wash and drain meat. Meanwhile, braise onions in heated oil until golden, 5–10 minutes. Add steak and kidneys and cook for about 30 minutes over medium heat, stirring frequently throughout cooking period. Add spices and cook a further 15 minutes. Add sago and cook until sago is transparent, about 15 minutes. Mix in grated egg if desired. Allow to cool before filling pies.
FILLS 75 PIES.

Chicken and Mushroom Filling

30 ml butter
1 onion, chopped
4 chicken breasts, skinned and boned
10 ml crushed garlic
salt and freshly ground black pepper to taste
2,5 ml ground cloves
150 g mushrooms, sliced
150 ml frozen, diced carrots
75 ml sago, soaked in 125 ml water

Heat butter and sauté onion until transparent. Cube chicken and add to onion together with garlic, salt, pepper and cloves and cook for 15 minutes. Add mushrooms and carrots and cook a further 5 minutes. Add soaked sago and cook until sago is transparent. Allow to cool before filling pies.
FILLS 50 PIES.

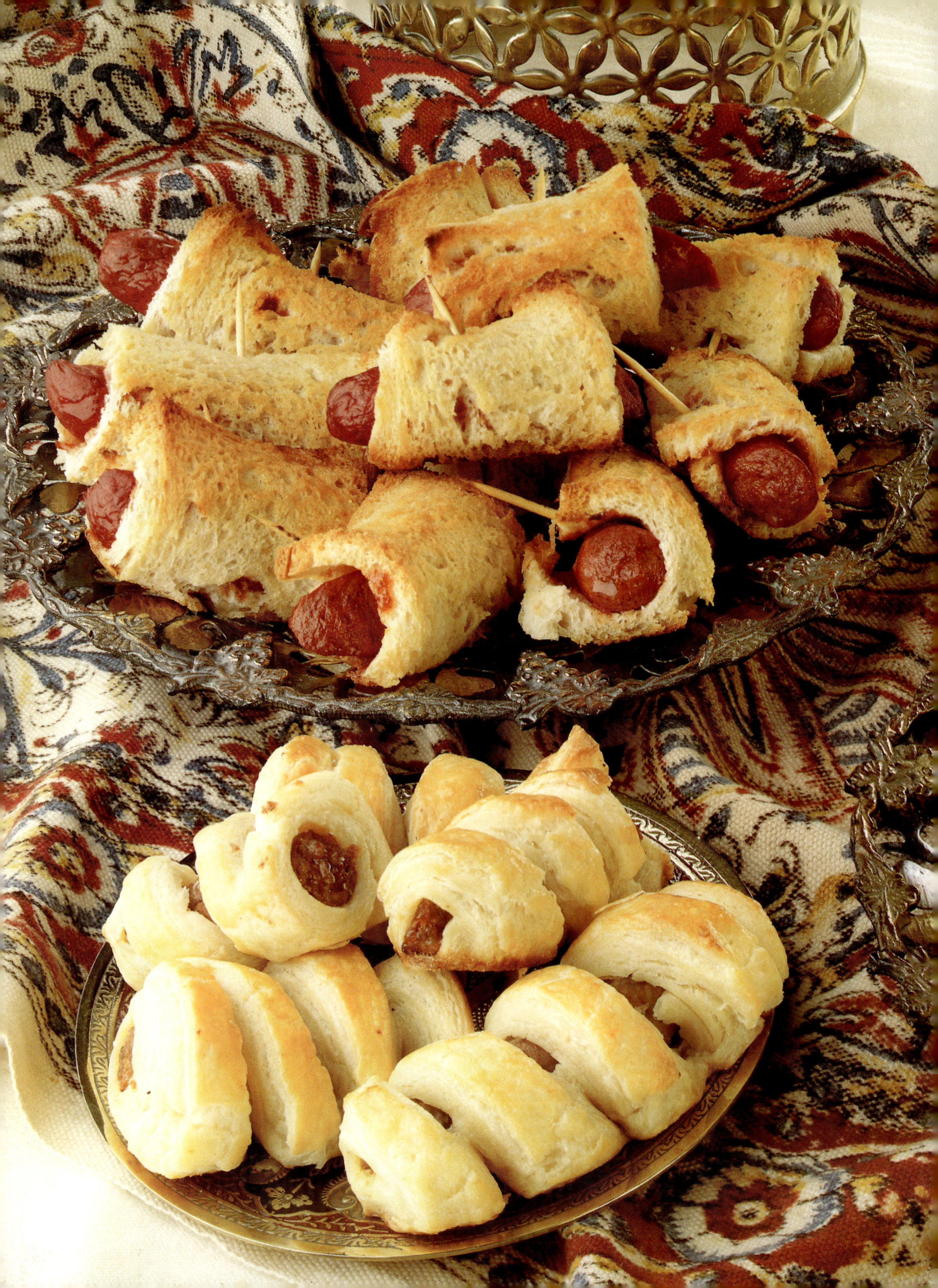

Clockwise from front left: Sausage ropes, Polony wrappers, Spicy roasted nuts and Gevulde nessies with Prawn filling and Chicken liver filling.

GEVULDE NESSIES

The fillings of these tender light cases of puff pastry may also be interchanged with any of the samoosa or savoury fillings.

**2 kg puff pastry (page 12)
1 egg, lightly beaten**

Preheat oven to 230 °C. Roll out puff pastry (page 12) to thickness of 1 cm. Cut out rounds using a 7,5 cm plain cutter and place them on a greased baking sheet. Using a 6 cm plain cutter, cut part of the way through the pastry in the centre of each round to mark the lids. Brush the tops with beaten egg and bake for about 10 minutes or until golden. Remove the lids with the point of a knife, scoop out any soft pastry from the centres and place the cases and lids on a wire rack to cool. Fill pastry cases with warm savoury fillings of choice.
MAKES 100 CASES.

Sheep Brain Filling

**4 sets sheep brains
20 ml cooking oil
10 ml butter
1 medium onion, finely chopped
salt to taste
1 green chilli, finely chopped**

Wash sheep brains very well under cold water and leave to soak. Heat oil and butter together and sauté onion until golden brown, about 10 minutes. Add sheep brains and cook for about 5 minutes, stirring all the time. Add salt and chilli and cook a further 3–5 minutes. Mixture should be fairly loose and soft, resembling scrambled eggs. Fill warm pastry cases and serve immediately.
FILLS ABOUT 30 CASES.

Prawn Filling

**200 g prawns, shelled and deveined
60 ml mayonnaise
60 ml tomato sauce
60 ml fresh cream
salt and pepper to taste
5 ml paprika
1 small onion, finely grated
sprigs of parsley for garnishing**

Cook prawns in lightly salted water for about 3 minutes, or until they turn pink in colour. Drain and set aside to cool. Mix together the remaining ingredients and combine with prawns. Spoon the mixture into cooled pastry cases and garnish with parsley.
FILLS ABOUT 36 CASES.

Chicken Liver Filling

**30 ml cooking oil
15 ml butter
1 medium onion, chopped
2,5 ml salt (or to taste)
5 ml coarsely ground black pepper
5 ml crushed garlic
5 ml crushed, dried red chillies
20 ml brown vinegar
10 ml sugar
300 g chicken livers**

Heat oil and butter together and sauté onion until transparent, about 5 minutes. Meanwhile, combine rest of ingredients, then add mixture to onion and cook a further 10 minutes, stirring all the time. Spoon filling into warm pastry cases and serve.
FILLS ABOUT 36 CASES.

BREAD CUPS

Bread cups take only a few minutes to prepare and are lovely for breakfast or as a starter at formal dinners, filled with any of the samoosa or savoury fillings. The cases can be made well in advance and can be stored in an airtight container to keep them crispy.

**24 slices white or brown bread, crusts removed
110 g butter or margarine, melted**

Preheat oven to 200 °C. Brush bread slices with melted butter. Line well-greased muffin or deep patty pans with bread slices, buttered sides up. Bake for 10–12 minutes or until crisp. Serve hot with fillings of your choice.
MAKES 24 BREAD CUPS.

POLONY WRAPPERS

A quick and easy snack, especially popular with kids. Can also be served for **soehr** *– the meal served early in the morning at the start of a fast.*

**12 slices white bread, crusts removed
60 ml tomato chutney or tomato sauce
6 Vienna sausages, cut in half
melted butter for brushing**

Preheat oven to 200 °C. Spread each bread slice with about 5 ml chutney. Wrap a slice of bread around each Vienna half, securing with a toothpick. Brush with melted butter. Place on a greased baking sheet and bake for 10 minutes or until bread is crisp and golden.
MAKES 12 WRAPPERS.

SAUSAGE ROPES

These very attractive snacks, served hot with chilli sauce or chutney, are ideal for special occasions or to send to neighbours and friends during Ramadan at the breaking of fast.

**500 g mutton or beef sausage
30 ml water
600 g puff pastry (page 12)
1 egg, lightly beaten**

Preheat oven to 230 °C. Wash sausage in cold water and leave to soak for about 15 minutes to prevent skin from popping. Steam sausage in about 30 ml water for 10 minutes, set aside to cool then cut into 6 cm pieces. Roll out pastry fairly thinly and cut into long strips about 1 cm wide. Wind a pastry strip around each sausage, leaving a little space between each winding. Place sausage ropes on a baking sheet in the freezer for about 10 minutes. Brush with egg, then bake for 10 minutes.
MAKES ABOUT 36 SAUSAGE ROPES.

KEBABS WITH CHUTNEY DIP

These spicy hot meatball kebabs, served with a tangy chutney dip, are ideal for entertaining.

**500 g steak mince
5 ml crushed garlic
10 ml crushed green chillies
5 ml freshly ground black pepper
5 ml salt
5 ml ground jeera (cumin)
1 onion, grated and juice squeezed out
1 egg, beaten
125 ml dried breadcrumbs
125 ml chopped dhunia (coriander) leaves
250 ml cooking oil for deep-frying**

CHUTNEY DIP
**60 ml peri-peri sauce
60 ml tomato chutney
60 ml fruit chutney**

Wash mince well and leave in a colander to drain. Mix drained mince with garlic, chillies, pepper, salt, jeera, onion and egg in a mixing bowl. Add breadcrumbs and dhunia leaves and mix until well blended. Form into small balls and deep-fry in heated oil until golden brown. Drain in a colander lined with paper towel. Insert a toothpick into each ball. For the dip, combine peri-peri sauce and chutneys and heat for about 5 minutes while stirring. Serve kebabs hot, and dipped into chutney dip.
MAKES 24 KEBABS.

DHALTJIES

Dhaltjies, also known as chilli bites, originated in India and are favourite Ramadan snacks among Cape Malays. These are sometimes served dipped into soup.

**250 ml pea or chana (yellow pea) flour
30 ml cake flour
1 onion, grated
5 ml ground jeera (cumin)
5 ml ground koljander (coriander)
10 ml crushed, dried red chillies
5 ml salt
2,5 ml borrie (turmeric)
½ bunch chopped dhunia (coriander) leaves
1 small green apple, grated
a few spinach leaves, shredded
5 ml baking powder
500 ml cooking oil for deep-frying**

Sift pea and cake flour into a fairly large mixing bowl. Add remaining ingredients, except baking powder and oil, and mix with sufficient water to make a thick batter. Stir in baking powder just before frying. Heat oil in a deep frying pan. Drop 15 ml batter at a time into hot oil and fry until lightly browned, about 5 minutes. Turn over and brown other side. Drain on paper towel and serve hot.
MAKES 24 DHALTJIES.

VARIATIONS
Bhajias (spinach leaves fried in chilli batter): Omit the grated apple and instead of shredding the spinach leaves, break them into 6 cm squares. Dip into batter and shallow-fry in hot oil on both sides until crisp, about 10 minutes. Drain on paper towel and serve hot.
Sweetcorn dhaltjies: Use 250 ml creamed sweetcorn instead of the apple.
Chilli chicken or kingklip: Omit apple, dhunia leaves and spinach. Dip chicken or kingklip portions into chilli batter and fry in medium-hot oil.

SPICY ROASTED NUTS

These nuts may be roasted in the oven or shallow-fried in cooking oil.

**1 x 500 g packet mixed nuts
5 ml salt
2,5 ml paprika
2,5 ml peri-peri powder**

Preheat oven to 220 °C. Spread nuts on a baking sheet and bake for about 5–10 minutes, turning nuts frequently to avoid burning. Pour nuts into a deep mixing bowl and sprinkle with salt and spices, coating all the nuts evenly.

Front: Seafood Akhni. Back: Grilled crayfish tail.

18 • *MORE CAPE MALAY COOKING*

SEAFOOD

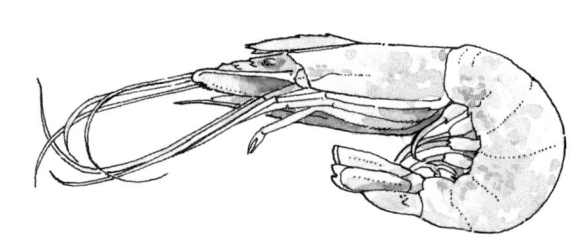

The Cape waters are enriched with a generous variety of fish. I can remember when the fish market in District Six was the hub of activity, especially on a Monday when the fish in season could be bought fresh.
Fish has always been very popular with Cape Malays and nowadays, owing to the trend in society, crayfish, prawns, perlemoen and calamari are delicacies enjoyed by many people. For this reason, I have included a variety of shellfish dishes such as Crayfish breyani, Perlemoen frikkadels, Prawn curry and Smoored skate wings. Contrary to Western traditions, it is common in Cape Malay cooking to serve a meal consisting of seafood snacks, a seafood starter and a seafood main course. It is always best to buy seafood fresh and to keep it refrigerated until required. A freshly caught fish can be recognized by its clear, bulging eyes, glittering scales and firm flesh. When preparing seafood, remember that the delicate flesh of most shellfish does not stand up to too much cooking, as it tends to toughen and lose flavour.

CRAYFISH COCKTAIL

A favourite starter at formal dinners, served with Malaysian prawns (page 20) as a main course.

5 cooked crayfish tails
1 onion, finely chopped
3 lettuce leaves, shredded
50 ml mayonnaise
30 ml tomato sauce
5 ml paprika
2,5 ml salt
15 drops Tabasco sauce
lettuce leaves and sliced cucumber and hard-boiled egg for garnishing

Shell, devein and cut crayfish into small cubes. Combine with rest of ingredients and mix well. Serve in cocktail bowls lined with lettuce leaves. Garnish with cucumber and egg.
SERVES 10 AS A STARTER.

VARIATION
For a more economical starter, cook 300 g filleted kingklip and crayfish together, then proceed as above.

GRILLED CRAYFISH TAILS

Crayfish tails may be grilled on an open fire or in the oven.

6 crayfish tails
100 g butter, melted
45 ml fresh lemon juice
45 ml honey
30 ml freshly chopped chives
10 ml paprika

Cut soft fins and shell away from crayfish tails, and rinse and drain well. Combine butter with rest of ingredients. Basting frequently with butter mixture, grill crayfish tails on open fire or in oven preheated to 230 °C until cooked and tender. Serve with savoury rice.
SERVES 6.

VARIATION
Grilled snoek: Substitute crayfish tails with well-cleaned snoek portions, and freshly chopped chives with 5 ml peri-peri powder. Brush snoek portions with butter mixture and grill as for crayfish.

CRAYFISH BREYANI

Breyani is a popular Indian and Cape Malay dish, usually served on special occasions. Crayfish breyani in particular, is an expensive dish served at Eid or when entertaining special guests.

1 kg crayfish tails
110 ml cooking oil or butter
2 large onions, finely sliced
500 ml uncooked rice
10 ml salt
pinch of borrie (turmeric)
100 ml water

MASALA MARINADE
10 ml crushed garlic
2 whole green chillies
5 ml salt (or to taste)
5 ml ground jeera (cumin)
125 ml tomato purée
100 ml natural yoghurt or buttermilk
2,5 ml borrie (turmeric)
5 ml crushed, dried red chillies
60 ml chopped dhunia (coriander) leaves
3 pieces stick cinnamon
3 cardamom pods
3 whole cloves

Shell crayfish and remove veins. Wash and drain well. Heat 50 ml oil or butter and braise crayfish until pale pink in colour. Remove crayfish and set aside. In same saucepan heat 60 ml oil and fry onions until crisp and golden brown. Meanwhile, boil well-washed rice in salted water with borrie until nearly done, rinse and drain. Rice must be *al dente* (firm). Combine marinade ingredients and add crayfish and onions. Place the marinating crayfish in a large saucepan and spread rice over. Garnish with fried onion and sprinkle 100 ml water over rice. Steam over low heat until crayfish is cooked and all the liquid has evaporated, about 35–45 minutes. Alternatively, use a large casserole dish and bake crayfish at 160 °C for about 1 hour.
SERVES 6.

VARIATION
Prawn breyani: Substitute crayfish with 1 kg prawns.

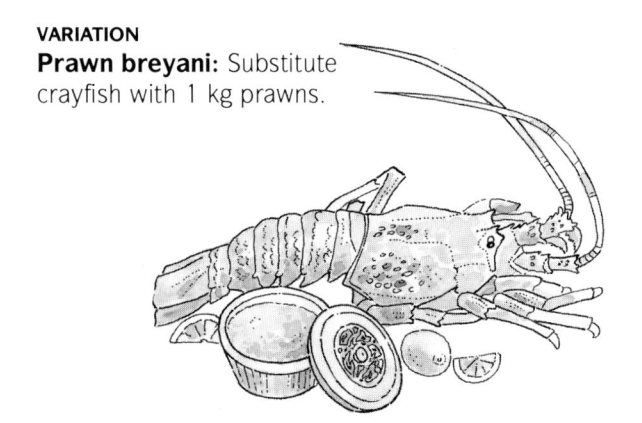

STIR-FRIED PRAWNS

A quick and easy dish which can be served with savoury rice and salads.

500 g prawns, shelled and deveined
5 ml salt
5 ml white pepper
5 ml paprika
45 ml cooking oil
lemon juice
lemon wedges for garnishing

Wash and drain prawns, then sprinkle with salt, pepper and paprika. Heat oil in a frying pan over moderate heat and stir-fry prawns for about 5 minutes. Before serving, season with lemon juice and garnish with lemon wedges.
SERVES 4.

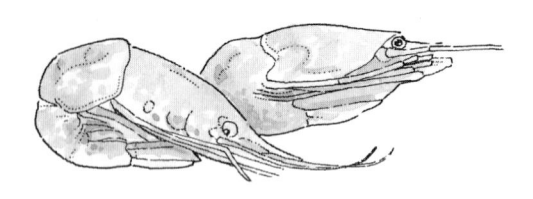

MALAYSIAN PRAWNS

Served on a bed of rice, these hot and spicy prawns with a tangy sauce are perfect for a main course, with Crayfish cocktail (page 19) as a starter.

1 medium onion, chopped
50 ml butter or margarine
½ green pepper, seeded and chopped
30 ml chopped celery
1 x 410 g can whole tomatoes
1 x 110 g can tomato paste
250 ml water
30 ml cake flour
20 ml dried mixed herbs
10 ml sugar
5 ml salt
5 ml chilli powder
2,5 ml freshly ground black pepper
500 g raw prawns, shelled and deveined

Sauté onion in heated butter until transparent. Add green pepper and celery and cook a further 5 minutes. Add whole tomatoes, tomato paste, water and flour and mix well. Cook for about 5 minutes over medium heat. Mix in remaining ingredients, except prawns, and cook for about 10 minutes. Add prawns and cook until prawns are tender, 5–10 minutes. Do not overcook, as prawns will become tough.
SERVES 6.

PRAWN CURRY

A lovely Indian curry which can be served with white rice and sambals.

500 g prawns, shelled and deveined
cooking oil for frying
1 large onion, finely sliced
125 ml skinned and grated tomato
50 ml natural yoghurt
1 green chilli, finely chopped
5 ml borrie (turmeric)
10 ml grated coconut or coconut milk
10 ml crushed garlic
5 ml salt
5 ml ground jeera (cumin)
5 ml ground koljander (coriander)
2,5 ml chilli powder
60 ml water
2,5 ml garam masala
curry leaves for garnishing

Wash prawns well and drain in colander. Braise prawns in a little oil until they turn pink in colour. In another saucepan, heat oil and fry onions until golden brown, 5–10 minutes. Add tomato and remaining ingredients, except prawns, water and garam masala, and cook for about 15 minutes or until gravy is thick. Add prawns and water to gravy and cook a further 10 minutes. Five minutes before cooking is complete, mix in the garam masala. Serve on a bed of white rice and garnished with curry leaves.
SERVES 4–6.

VARIATION
Crayfish curry: Use 500 g shelled, deveined and cubed crayfish instead of prawns.
Fish curry: Any fresh fish such as red roman, yellowtail or kingklip can be used in the place of the prawns to make a delicious fish curry.

PRAWN CUTLETS

These butterfly-shaped prawns can also be served on a bed of lettuce leaves as a starter to Minced perlemoen curry (page 24).

20 extra-large prawns
2 large onions, grated
5 ml grated fresh root ginger
5 ml chilli powder
5 ml salt (or to taste)
2 eggs, lightly beaten
250 ml cake flour
250 ml dried breadcrumbs
cooking oil for shallow-frying

Remove prawns from shells but keep tails intact. Slit prawns down back and remove vein. Wash and drain well. Flatten prawns slightly. Combine onions, ginger, chilli powder and salt to form a paste. Smear paste over flattened prawns and allow to marinate for 30 minutes. Dust marinated prawns with flour, dip into egg and coat with breadcrumbs. Fry on both sides in shallow oil until cooked through. Serve with hot potato chips and salad.
SERVES 4 AS A MAIN COURSE AND 10 AS A STARTER.

SEAFOOD AKHNI

A modern breyani prepared like paella, which can be served at Eid or on any special occasion.

1 kg mixed seafood (prawns, calamari, kingklip and crayfish tails)
3 large onions, finely sliced
cooking oil for frying
200 g mushrooms, chopped
1 green pepper, seeded and chopped
1 red pepper, seeded and chopped
750 ml uncooked rice
salt and Tabasco sauce to taste

MARINADE
60 ml peri-peri sauce
10 ml crushed garlic
salt and freshly ground black pepper to taste
5 ml Tabasco sauce

Combine marinade ingredients in a mixing bowl, add mixed seafood and marinate for about 1 hour. Meanwhile, fry onions in heated oil until golden, 5–10 minutes. Add mushrooms and fry a further 5–10 minutes, or until softened. Remove onions and mushrooms from pan and set aside. Fry peppers in oil for 5 minutes, remove from pan and set aside. Transfer seafood and marinade to frying pan and fry for 15 minutes. Meanwhile, boil rice in salted water until tender, about 20 minutes. Drain and rinse. Layer ingredients in a large saucepan as follows: first rice, then onions and mushrooms (reserving some onion for garnishing), then peppers, and finally the seafood mixture. Continue layering until all ingredients have been used up, sprinkling each layer with a little salt and Tabasco sauce. Steam, covered, over medium heat for 30 minutes. Garnish with reserved onions. Serve on its own or as an accompaniment to Prawn curry.
SERVES 6–8.

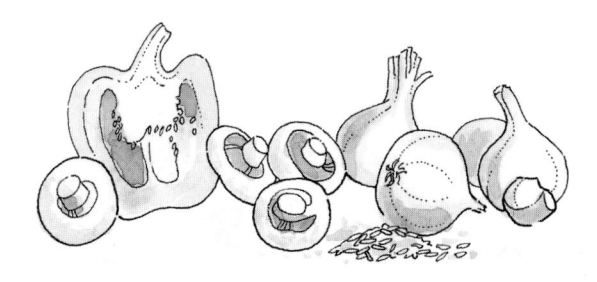

SEAFOOD • 21

*Back row, left to right: Deep-fried calamari rings, Perlemoen frikkadels, Prawn cutlets, Prawn curry and braised rice.
Front row, left to right: Dhal sauce with braised onion and Dry spicy masala fish.*

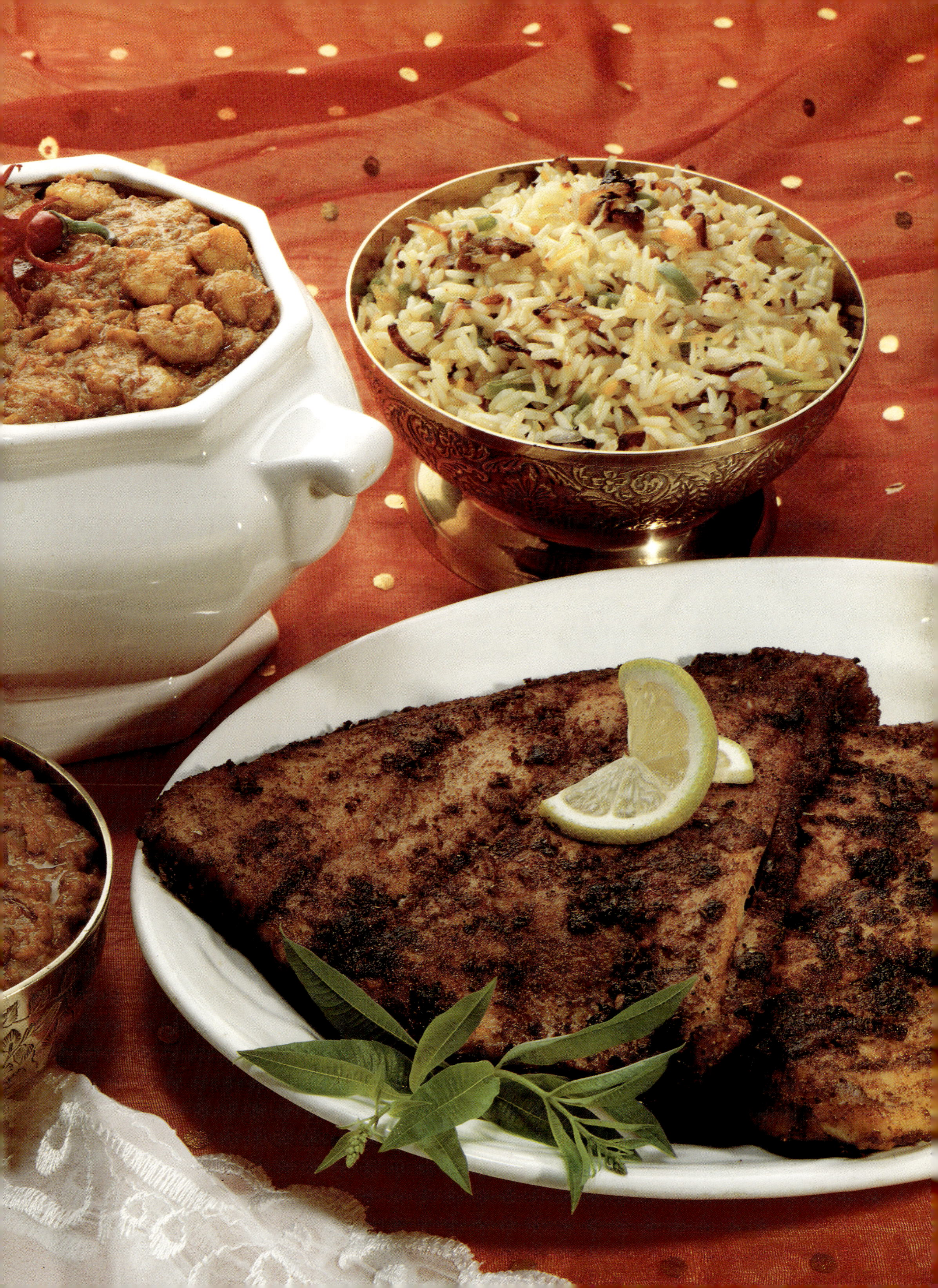

MINCED PERLEMOEN CURRY

At first glance, this dish looks very much like mince curry, so serve it in perlemoen shells so as not to confuse your guests. As a variation, octopus can be substituted for the perlemoen.

1 kg well-washed and scrubbed perlemoen
30 ml cooking oil
3 large onions, thinly sliced
10 ml crushed garlic
1 tomato, grated
5 ml borrie (turmeric)
5 ml ground koljander (coriander)
5 ml ground jeera (cumin)
4 bay leaves
1 green chilli, finely chopped
a few strands saffron (optional)
10 ml roasted masala
salt to taste
5 ml sugar
125 ml water

Mince perlemoen and set aside. Heat oil in a heavy-based saucepan and braise onions and garlic until golden brown, 5–10 minutes. Add tomato, spices, sugar and water to make a thick gravy. Cook, covered, for about 10 minutes, stirring frequently. Add perlemoen and cook a further 30 minutes until well blended. Serve on a bed of white rice.
SERVES 8–10.

DRY SPICY MASALA FISH

A very dry but delicious fish dish, best served smothered in Dhal sauce with braised onion (page 44).

5 ml chilli powder
5 ml ground jeera (cumin)
5 ml freshly ground black pepper
10 ml crushed garlic
5 ml garam masala
1 green chilli, crushed
10 ml chopped dhunia (coriander) leaves
20 ml lemon juice
1 kg filleted kingklip, hake or gurnards
cooking oil for shallow-frying

Combine spices, dhunia leaves and lemon juice and rub into fish fillets. Set aside to marinate for 15–20 minutes. Heat oil in a heavy-based frying pan and fry fish for about 5 minutes on each side. Keep cooked fillets warm while frying the rest. Alternatively, place fillets in a baking tray, brush with oil and grill or bake in a preheated oven at 180 °C for about 15 minutes. Serve with lemon slices.
SERVES 4.

PERLEMOEN FRIKKADELS

Perlemoen frikkadels can also be served as a snack or starter by simply shaping them into cocktail-sized balls before frying.

500 g perlemoen, cleaned
1 onion, thinly sliced
2 slices bread, soaked in water and moisture squeezed out
1 egg, beaten
5 ml salt
5 ml freshly ground black pepper
5 ml grated nutmeg
30 ml freshly chopped parsley
1 ripe tomato, skinned and grated
10 ml crushed garlic
cooking oil for shallow-frying

Cut perlemoen into steaks and beat with a mallet to tenderize, then mince. Combine all ingredients, except oil, in large bowl and mix to bind well. Shape into frikkadels and shallow-fry in medium-hot oil for about 5 minutes each side, or until lightly browned. Serve hot with Dhal sauce with braised onion (page 44), white rice and blatjang.
SERVES 4 AS A MAIN COURSE.

FISH FRIKKADELS

An economical dish with a slightly smoky flavour. Traditionally served on a Monday after the rich spicy foods eaten during the weekend.

250 g hake fillets
250 g haddock fillets
3 slices stale bread
45 ml freshly chopped parsley
5 ml freshly grated black pepper
1 egg, lightly beaten
2,5 ml grated nutmeg
cooking oil for shallow-frying

Poach hake and haddock fillets in water for about 10 minutes, drain well and flake. Soak bread in water for 5 minutes, then squeeze out all the moisture. Combine flaked fish and bread with rest of ingredients and shape into flat cakes. Shallow-fry in hot oil until brown and crisp, about 5 minutes on each side. Serve the frikkadels hot with blatjang or *gesmoorde* tomato and onion sauce.
SERVES 4.

VARIATION
Add 125 ml skinned and grated tomato and 5 ml ground jeera to the frikkadel mixture before shaping into flat cakes and shallow-frying as above.

SMOORED SKATE WINGS

A quick and easy dish ideal for a light lunch.

30 ml cooking oil
1 large onion, thinly sliced
2 tomatoes, skinned and grated
10 ml crushed garlic
5 ml salt
5 ml crushed, dried red chillies
5 ml sugar (or to taste)
500 g fresh skate wings,
cleaned and cut into chunks

Heat oil in large saucepan and sauté onion until golden, 5–10 minutes. Add tomatoes and simmer for about 10 minutes. Add garlic, salt, chilli and sugar, and cook until sauce is well blended, about 10 minutes. Add skate wings and simmer, covered, over medium heat for 15 minutes. Serve on a bed of white rice.
SERVES 6.

VARIATION
Smoored snoek roe: Use 500 g snoek roe instead of skate wings and proceed as above.

DEEP-FRIED CALAMARI RINGS

These crunchy calamari rings are best served on a bed of savoury rice.

500 g calamari rings
100 ml fresh lemon juice
10 ml crushed garlic
250 ml cake flour
5 ml salt
5 ml freshly ground black pepper
1 egg, well beaten
20 ml fresh milk
250 ml dried breadcrumbs
5 ml dried mixed herbs
500 ml cooking oil for deep-frying

Wash and drain calamari rings. Marinate calamari rings in lemon juice and garlic for about 30 minutes. Meanwhile, combine flour, salt and pepper in a mixing bowl. In another bowl, mix egg and milk. Place breadcrumbs and mixed herbs in a paper or plastic bag and shake to blend. Dust marinated calamari rings with flour mixture, dip into egg and milk mixture, and coat with breadcrumbs. Heat oil in a deep saucepan. Drop calamari rings into deep, hot oil, a small batch at a time, and fry 1–2 minutes or until golden brown. Remove from oil with a slotted spoon and drain on paper towel. Serve hot, garnished with lemon wedges.
SERVES 4.

FRIED SNOEK ROE

This very neglected and often discarded part of the snoek is ideal as a starter served with chutney.

500 g snoek roe
5 ml salt
2,5 ml freshly ground black pepper
2,5 ml chilli powder
1 egg, lightly beaten
cooking oil for shallow-frying

Boil snoek roe until set, about 10 minutes. Allow to cool, then cut into 7-cm-long pieces. Sprinkle with salt, pepper and chilli powder. Dip into beaten egg and shallow-fry until golden. Drain on paper towel.
SERVES 8 AS A STARTER.

STOKVIS BOBOTIE

A delicious hake bobotie which can be varied by using any type of white fish.

15 ml butter
15 ml cooking oil
2 onions, thinly sliced
5 ml crushed, dried red chillies
15 ml garam masala
30 ml fresh lemon juice
5 ml salt
1 kg minced hake
3 slices stale bread
250 ml milk
50 ml chopped dhunia (coriander) leaves
1 egg, lightly beaten

TOPPING
125 ml milk
2 eggs, lightly beaten
5 ml paprika
pinch of salt
5 bay or lemon leaves
almonds for garnishing

Heat butter and oil in a frying pan. Add onions and sauté until transparent. Transfer onions to a large mixing bowl and add chillies, garam masala, lemon juice, salt and minced hake and mix well. Meanwhile, soak bread in milk, then squeeze out excess milk. Add bread, dhunia leaves and egg to hake mixture, mix well and transfer to a greased ovenproof dish. Prepare topping by mixing together milk, eggs, paprika and salt. Pour topping over hake mixture and garnish with bay or lemon leaves and almonds. Bake, covered, for 30 minutes at 190 °C, then grill until golden, about 5 minutes.
SERVES 6-8.

Clockwise from back: Chicken giblet soup with paaper and Spicy chicken salad.

Chicken

Chicken has become very popular in recent years for a number of reasons. It is still the cheapest meat available, it is fast-cooking and it is a perfect choice if you prefer white to red meat. Chicken is also extremely versatile – it can be grilled, baked, pot-roasted, used in stews, soups and salads, as shown in the recipes given here. Furthermore, the wide availability of special cuts such as breasts, drumsticks and livers, makes chicken one of the most convenient of meats, the presentation of which may be as simple or as elaborate as you wish.

CHICKEN AKHNI

An easy way to serve curry and rice as all the ingredients are cooked in one saucepan so that the rice becomes moist and takes on the flavour of the curry.

500 ml uncooked rice
30 ml cooking oil
2 large onions, thinly sliced
1 kg chicken portions
1 green chilli, finely chopped
5 ml salt (or to taste)
10 ml grated fresh root ginger
10 ml crushed garlic
5 ml ground jeera (cumin)
5 ml ground koljander (coriander)
5 ml ground barishap (fennel)
5 ml borrie (turmeric)
5 ml chilli powder
5 whole cloves
3 cardamom seeds
3 pieces stick cinnamon
1 tomato, skinned and grated
5 potatoes, halved
200 ml hot water
60 ml chopped dhunia (coriander) leaves

Boil rice in salted water until just tender, about 15 minutes, then rinse and drain. Heat oil in a large saucepan and braise onions until golden, 5–10 minutes. Add chicken and spices and cook, covered, over medium heat until chicken is tender, about 30 minutes. Add tomato, potatoes and water and cook until potatoes are nearly tender, about 10 minutes. Mix in rice, then steam, covered, over low heat until well blended, about 20 minutes. Garnish with dhunia leaves and serve with atjars and sambals.

SERVES 8–10.

CHICKEN GIBLET SOUP

*Soup is traditionally served at **boeka** time (sunset) during Ramadan. For a crunchy effect, serve sprinkled with crushed paaper.*

500 g chicken giblets or necks
250 ml dried split peas, soaked overnight
5 whole cloves
3 whole allspice
2 litres water
1 bunch carrots, grated
2 leeks, finely chopped
1 large tomato, skinned and grated
1 large turnip, grated
50 ml chopped parsley
100 ml chopped celery
salt and freshly ground black pepper to taste

Cook well-washed and drained giblets, split peas, cloves and allspice in 1 litre water in a large saucepan until split peas are very soft, about 45 minutes. Add vegetables and remaining water and cook a further 30 minutes. Season with salt and pepper to taste and cook a further 15 minutes over medium heat.

SERVES 6.

VARIATION
- **Vegetable soup:** Omit the chicken giblets and proceed as above.
- Instead of 250 ml split peas, use 125 ml split peas and 125 ml red lentils.
- Substitute split peas with 250 ml barley.

Cook's tip
Do not discard the giblet packet in whole chicken. Clean, wash and freeze contents for later use.

SPICY CHICKEN SALAD

A quick, easy and very tasty way to use up leftover chicken. This salad can be served as a starter or as a light meal.

250 g cooked chicken meat, shredded
1 large tomato, skinned and chopped
5 ml freshly ground black pepper
10 ml garlic steak seasoning
½ English cucumber, sliced
½ lettuce, finely shredded
1 small onion, peeled and thinly sliced
½ green pepper, cored, seeded and thinly sliced
25 ml chopped dhunia (coriander) leaves
5 ml jeera (cumin) seeds
juice of 1 lemon
pinch of salt

In a large bowl, combine chicken and remaining ingredients and mix well. To allow the flavours to blend, set aside for at least 30 minutes before serving.
SERVES 6 AS A STARTER AND 4 AS A LIGHT MEAL.

VARIATION
For a fruity variation, add to the salad 1 cored and chopped green apple and ½ peeled and chopped pineapple.

PAPRIKA POT-ROAST CHICKEN

Sundays are not the same without a pot-roast. Served with Almond yellow rice (page 81), this makes an ideal Sunday lunch.

1,5 kg chicken portions
10 ml garlic steak seasoning
10 ml paprika
5 ml peri-peri powder
30 ml tomato chutney
5 ml salt
60 ml melted butter or cooking oil
3 large potatoes, peeled and halved
250 g baby carrots
250 g baby sweetcorn

Clean, wash and drain chicken well. Prick each portion thoroughly with a fork and rub in spices, chutney and salt. Heat butter in a wide-based saucepan and brown chicken on all sides, about 15 minutes. Cover saucepan and steam a further 10 minutes. Pile chicken onto one side of saucepan, add potatoes, carrots and sweetcorn and cook, covered, until vegetables are soft, about 10–15 minutes. If pot-roast becomes too dry, add about 50 ml hot water.
SERVES 6.

TOMATO CHICKEN CURRY

The tomato makes this a very rich gravy curry, best served on a bed of savoury rice with salads.

45 ml cooking oil
1 large onion, thinly sliced
2 pieces stick cinnamon
3 cardamom pods
2 green chillies, halved and seeded
15 ml grated fresh root ginger
10 ml crushed garlic
8 chicken portions
10 ml ground jeera (cumin)
½ bunch chopped dhunia (coriander) leaves
1 x 410 g can whole tomatoes
5 ml salt (or to taste)

Heat cooking oil in a large saucepan, and fry onions until golden brown. Add the cinnamon, cardamom and green chillies and fry for 1 minute, then add the ginger and garlic and fry a further 1 minute. Add the chicken portions and cook for 15 minutes. Add the jeera and the dhunia leaves and cook for about 2 minutes. Stir in the tomatoes and salt. Cover and cook over low heat until chicken is tender, approximately 30–35 minutes.
SERVES 8.

MASALA CHICKEN WITH PRUNES

An ideal substitute for the cold chicken traditionally served at weddings.

1 x 1,5 kg chicken, quartered
1 x 250 g packet pitted prunes
10 ml crushed garlic
10 ml grated fresh root ginger
5 ml chilli powder
10 ml ground jeera (cumin)
10 ml ground koljander (coriander)
5 ml garam masala
10 ml paprika
7,5 ml salt (or to taste)
1 x 410 g can tomato purée
100 g butter
5 potatoes, peeled

Clean, wash and drain chicken. Combine with rest of ingredients, except butter and potatoes, and mix well. In a deep saucepan, heat butter and when hot add chicken quarters, leaving prunes and marinade in bowl. Marinate potatoes in prune and marinade mixture. Fry chicken until browned, about 15 minutes a side. Add marinade, prune and potato mixture and cook until potatoes are soft, about 15 minutes. Serve with white rice.
SERVES 6.

TANDOORI CHICKEN

This is a convenient lunch for a busy Sunday, because most of the preparation can be done the day before, as the chicken needs to marinate overnight for the flavours to develop.

1 x 1,5 kg chicken, cut into portions or halved
salt to taste
cooking oil for grilling

MARINADE
5 ml chilli powder
5 ml freshly ground black pepper
10 ml grated fresh root ginger or 5 ml ground ginger
10 ml crushed garlic
10 ml paprika
300 ml natural yoghurt
15 ml lemon juice
orange food colouring (optional)

Clean and wash chicken well and drain in colander. With a sharp knife, make slits through the chicken portions and rub in salt. Mix together marinade ingredients and marinate chicken portions, covered, for at least 12 hours. The longer it marinates, the better the result will be. Place chicken portions on a baking sheet and grill for about 15 minutes on each side, turning them regularly and brushing with oil every few minutes. Serve with fresh salad.
SERVES 4–6.

SPICY YOGHURT CHICKEN

1 x 1,5 kg chicken, cut into portions
50 ml butter or cooking oil
1 large onion, thinly sliced
10 ml crushed garlic
5 ml ground ginger
5 ml salt (or to taste)
750 ml hot water
450 ml natural yoghurt
½ bunch chopped dhunia (coriander) leaves
½ small green pepper, seeded and chopped
2,5 ml borrie (turmeric)
5 ml garam masala

Clean, wash and drain chicken very well. Heat butter and fry onion until golden brown. Mix in the garlic, ginger and salt and cook for 5 minutes. Add chicken portions and brown well. Add water and simmer for about 45 minutes, or until the chicken is tender and about 50 ml gravy remains. Mix in the yoghurt, dhunia leaves, green pepper, borrie and garam masala and stir thoroughly. Heat through without boiling, then serve with yellow rice and fresh salad.
SERVES 6.

CHICKEN BREYANI

Breyani is a dish of Indian origin adapted by the Cape Malays and usually served on special occasions such as weddings.

1,5 kg chicken portions
10 ml grated fresh root ginger
10 ml crushed garlic
5 ml salt (or to taste)
250 ml brown lentils
625 ml long-grain or basmati rice
250 ml cooking oil
300 ml hot water
7 potatoes, peeled and quartered
3 large onions, thinly sliced
1 small green pepper, cut into strips
50 g butter
6 hard-boiled eggs for garnishing

MARINADE
3 pieces stick cinnamon
5 cardamom seeds
2 green chillies, finely chopped
2,5 ml borrie (turmeric)
5 ml roasted masala
30 ml garam masala
5 whole cloves
5 whole allspice
a few strands saffron
1 large tomato, skinned and grated
250 ml buttermilk or natural yoghurt

Wash and drain chicken portions in colander. Combine ginger, garlic and salt and rub into meat. Mix together marinade ingredients and marinate meat for about 2 hours. Boil lentils until tender, about 20 minutes, then rinse and drain. Wash rice until water runs clear and drain well. Heat 50 ml cooking oil in large saucepan over medium heat, add rice and toss with slotted spoon to coat well. Add 100 ml hot water and cook, covered, for 5 minutes. Remove from stove. Heat remaining oil in large saucepan and fry potatoes until browned, about 3 minutes. Remove potatoes from saucepan and set aside. Add onion and green pepper to oil in saucepan and braise until brown and crisp, 7–10 minutes, reserving a quarter for later use. Add meat and spices to remaining onions and cook, covered, for 25 minutes. Remove meat from saucepan and keep warm. In the same saucepan, layer ingredients in the following order: potatoes, half the rice, the chicken mixture, lentils, the remaining rice, and lastly the reserved onions. Dot with butter and sprinkle with remaining hot water. Cook, covered, over high heat for 5 minutes, turn the heat down and simmer for 30–45 minutes. Garnish with halved hard-boiled eggs. Serve with atjars and sambals.
SERVES 12–15.

Cook's tip
Layer prepared ingredients in a casserole dish and cook, covered, in oven at 180 °C for 45–60 minutes.

CHICKEN • 29

CRUMBED CHICKEN BREASTS

Served hot or cold, these crumbed and deep-fried chicken breasts are ideal for a picnic.

6 small chicken breast fillets
10 ml crushed garlic
½ green pepper, crushed
10 ml salt
5 ml ground ginger
2 eggs, lightly beaten
250 ml cake flour
250 ml dried breadcrumbs
cooking oil for deep-frying

Flatten the fillets with a meat tenderizer. Mix the garlic, green pepper, salt and ginger together. Apply this mixture to both sides of the fillets. Refrigerate and allow to marinate for at least 6 hours. Dust chicken fillets with cake flour, dip into beaten egg and coat with breadcrumbs. Fry fillets two at a time in deep, moderately hot oil. Serve with hot potato chips and fresh salad.
SERVES 6.

Cook's tip
To test if oil is the right temperature, drop a small cube of bread into it. It should turn golden brown within 1 minute. The oil should not be too hot, otherwise the chicken will brown too much before being cooked through.

CHICKEN KEBABS

Although it is better to grill these kebabs on an open fire, they can also be grilled in an oven.

1 kg chicken breast fillets
5 ml salt
5 ml chilli powder
2,5 ml ground jeera (cumin)
5 ml freshly ground black pepper
juice of 1 lemon
5 ml grated lemon rind
1 green pepper, cubed
150 g fresh button mushrooms
100 g pickling onions, peeled and halved
30 ml cooking oil
30 ml butter, melted

Cube chicken breasts, wash and drain well. Combine chicken, seasonings, lemon juice and rind in a large bowl and mix well. Cover and allow to marinate for at least 3 hours. Thread chicken onto skewers alternating with green pepper, mushrooms and onions. Grill over open fire, basting with mixture of melted butter and oil. Serve with fresh salad.
SERVES 6.

CHICKEN TIKKA

A popular Cape Malay dish introduced by pilgrims from Mecca. These grilled spicy chicken pieces can be bought at street cafés all around Mecca and Medina.

1 chicken, quartered
5 ml salt (or to taste)
5 ml chilli powder
5 ml crushed garlic
5 ml grated fresh root ginger
15 ml fresh lemon juice
30 ml natural yoghurt
15 ml cooking oil
30 ml chopped chives for garnishing
1 lemon, sliced for garnishing

Clean and wash chicken quarters thoroughly, then drain well. Combine rest of ingredients in a small bowl. Make deep slits in chicken quarters and rub in marinade. Allow to marinate for about 3 hours. Grill chicken over charcoal or in oven at 200 °C for 15–20 minutes, turning pieces over frequently. Garnish with chopped chives and slices of lemon.
SERVES 6.

STIR-FRIED CHICKEN

A very quick and convenient meal to serve out of doors, as it can be cooked on a skottelbraai.

500 g chicken breast fillets
5 ml salt
15 ml peri-peri sauce
10 ml tomato chutney
5 ml crushed garlic
15 ml cooking oil
15 ml butter
250 ml shredded red cabbage
250 ml julienne carrots
125 ml finely chopped onion
250 ml sliced green pepper
50 ml chopped celery

Cut chicken into strips, wash and drain very well. Combine salt, sauce, chutney and garlic and rub into chicken strips. Heat oil and butter in a skottelbraai or wok, add chicken and quick-fry for 5–10 minutes, stirring all the time. Add all the vegetables and stir-fry another 10 minutes, or until vegetables are tender (must still be crispy). Serve immediately on a bed of white rice.
SERVES 6–8.

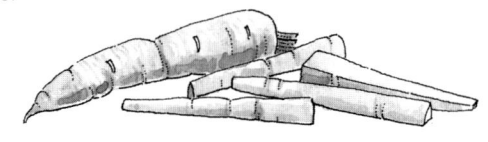

Clockwise from front: Masala chicken with prunes, Spicy yoghurt chicken and a mixed salad.

CHICKEN • 31

MEAT

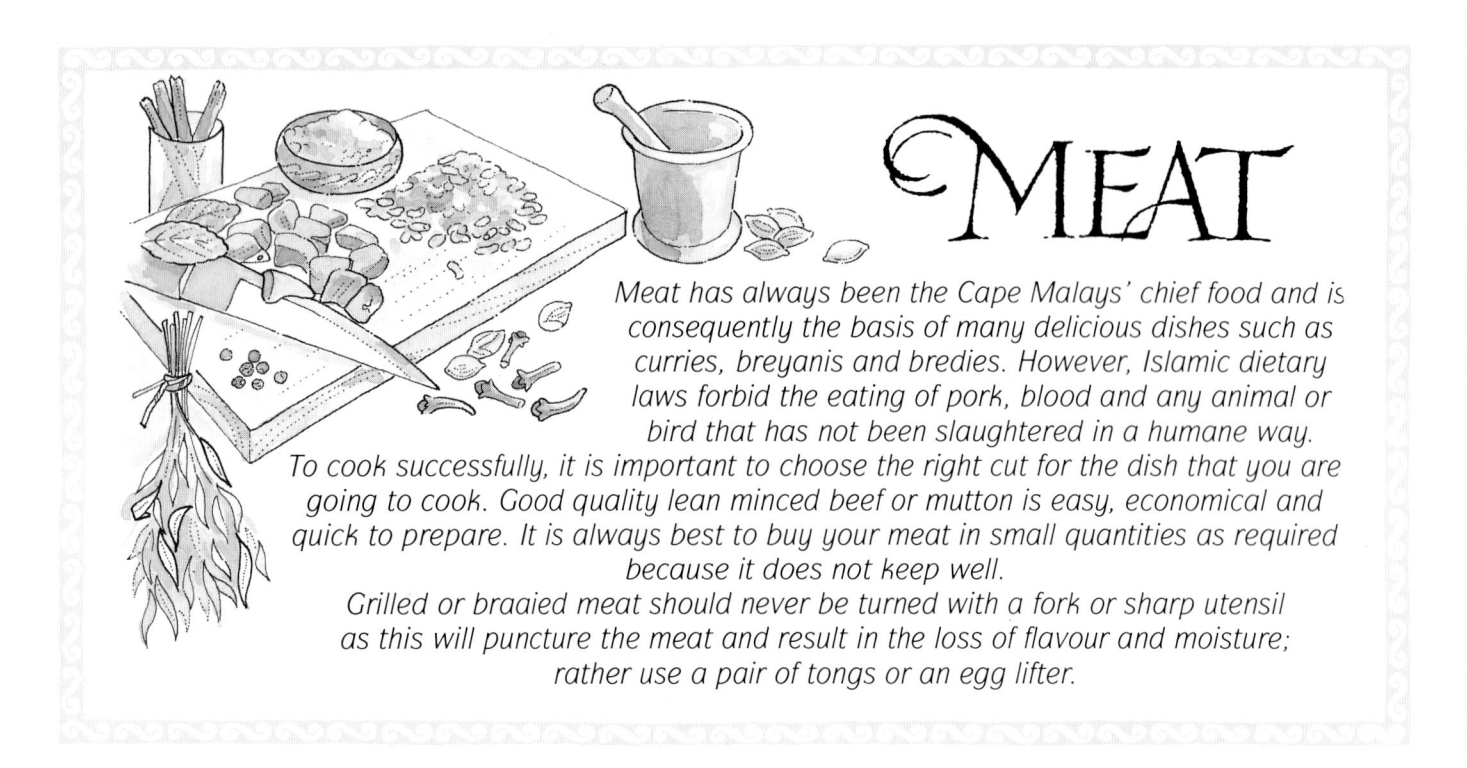

Meat has always been the Cape Malays' chief food and is consequently the basis of many delicious dishes such as curries, breyanis and bredies. However, Islamic dietary laws forbid the eating of pork, blood and any animal or bird that has not been slaughtered in a humane way.
To cook successfully, it is important to choose the right cut for the dish that you are going to cook. Good quality lean minced beef or mutton is easy, economical and quick to prepare. It is always best to buy your meat in small quantities as required because it does not keep well.
Grilled or braaied meat should never be turned with a fork or sharp utensil as this will puncture the meat and result in the loss of flavour and moisture; rather use a pair of tongs or an egg lifter.

MUTTON AND VEGETABLE STEW

An updated version of the traditional carrot and pea or sago stew.

30 ml cooking oil
2 onions, thinly sliced
600 g mutton or lamb, cubed
5 whole cloves
5 whole allspice
5 ml salt (or to taste)
10 ml crushed, dried red chillies
2,5 ml grated nutmeg
10 ml sugar
500 ml frozen mixed vegetables
150 ml water

Heat oil in large saucepan and braise onions until golden, 5–10 minutes. Add well-washed and drained meat, cover and braise slowly for approximately 30 minutes or until meat is fairly tender. Add cloves, allspice, salt, chillies and nutmeg and cook, uncovered, over high heat for about 10 minutes or until meat has browned well, adding sugar to help the browning. Add frozen mixed vegetables and water and cook, covered, over moderate heat for about 15 minutes. Serve on a bed of white rice.
SERVES 6.

VARIATION
Soak 125 ml sago in 250 ml water for 15 minutes. Add to stew after adding frozen vegetables and cook, covered, over low heat until sago is transparent, about 15 minutes. Serve with Mashed potatoes (page 83).

LAMB AND TOMATO CURRY

30 ml cooking oil
3 large onions, thinly sliced
1 x 1 kg leg of lamb, cut into chunks
10 ml crushed garlic
15 ml grated fresh root ginger
1 green chilli, finely chopped
3 pieces stick cinnamon
5 cardamom pods
5 whole cloves
5 ml ground jeera (cumin)
5 ml ground koljander (coriander)
15 ml roasted masala
5 ml borrie (turmeric)
5 ml salt (or to taste)
150 ml water
500 ml grated tomato
5 ml sugar
30 ml tomato paste
12 baby potatoes, peeled
60 ml chopped dhunia (coriander) leaves

Heat oil in a large saucepan and braise onions until golden brown, about 10 minutes. Add meat, garlic, ginger, chilli, stick cinnamon, cardamom and cloves and braise, covered, for about 30 minutes. Add spices and cook a further 15 minutes, stirring frequently. Mix in rest of ingredients, except potatoes and dhunia leaves, and cook a further 15 minutes over moderate heat. Add potatoes and cook until soft, about 15 minutes. Stir in dhunia leaves. Serve with Indian puris (page 84) or white rice, atjars and sambals.
SERVES 6–8.

MALAYSIAN-STYLE BEEF

The cucumber balances this otherwise hot and spicy dish.

750 g sirloin steak, cut into 2 cm x 7 cm strips
2,5 ml white pepper
2,5 ml ground cinnamon
2,5 ml ground cloves
7,5 ml salt (or to taste)
5 ml sugar
50 ml cooking oil
1 large onion, thinly sliced
15 ml grated fresh root ginger
15 ml chilli sauce (optional)
75 ml water
30 ml soy sauce
15 ml chopped dhunia (coriander) leaves
½ English cucumber, peeled and diced (optional)

In a large bowl, marinate beef in mixture of white pepper, cinnamon, ground cloves, salt and sugar. Heat oil in large saucepan, add onion and fry until golden brown. Stir in marinated beef, ginger, chilli sauce and water and bring to the boil. Reduce heat and simmer, covered, for about 1 hour or until meat is tender. Remove lid, add soy sauce and simmer until gravy is thick. Stir in dhunia leaves and cucumber, if using. Serve with white rice and fresh vegetable salads.
SERVES 6–8.

TOMATO FRIKKADEL BREDIE

30 ml cooking oil
2 large onions, thinly sliced
1 kg mutton knuckles, or chopped neck
1 kg ripe tomatoes, skinned and grated or puréed
10 ml crushed garlic
5 ml salt (or to taste)
5 ml crushed, dried red chilli
30 ml sugar (or to taste)
15 ml tomato paste

FRIKKADELS
500 g steak mince
5 ml white pepper
5 ml salt
5 ml crushed garlic
2,5 ml grated nutmeg
1 egg

Heat oil in a large saucepan and braise onions until golden, 5–10 minutes. Add meat and braise, covered, over medium heat for 30 minutes. Add tomatoes, garlic, salt and chilli and simmer a further 15 minutes. Stir in sugar and tomato paste and simmer for 5 minutes. Combine frikkadel ingredients, shape into balls then add to tomato mixture and cook for 15 minutes. Serve hot with white rice.
SERVES 10.

MINCE CURRY WITH BRINJALS

500 g steak mince
30 ml cooking oil
2 large onions, sliced
1 tomato, skinned and grated
15 ml grated fresh root ginger
10 ml crushed garlic
3 pieces stick cinnamon
5 cardamom seeds, lightly bruised
3 whole cloves
10 ml roasted masala
5 ml borrie (turmeric)
5 ml ground jeera (cumin)
5 ml ground koljander (coriander)
1 green chilli, finely chopped
1 large brinjal, cubed

Wash and drain mince. Heat oil in saucepan and sauté onions until transparent. Add tomato and cook for 10 minutes. Add all the spices and simmer until well blended, about 15 minutes. Crumble mince into sauce and cook, covered, for 30 minutes. Meanwhile, soak brinjal in lightly salted water for 15 minutes, then drain. Add brinjal to mince mixture and cook a further 10 minutes. Serve hot with rotis and atjars.
SERVES 4–6.

POT-ROAST MASALA LEG CHOPS

A saucy alternative to pot-roast leg of lamb which is traditionally served for Sunday lunch.

1 kg mutton leg chops
5 ml salt
5 ml freshly ground black pepper
15 ml roasted masala or red leaf masala
60 ml cooking oil
60 ml tomato sauce
60 ml peri-peri sauce
125 ml hot water
12 large pitted prunes
8 baby potatoes, peeled
250 g baby carrots, peeled

Wash and drain meat. Sprinkle with salt, black pepper and 10 ml masala. In a deep saucepan, fry meat in heated oil until tender and browned, 35–40 minutes. In a bowl mix together sauces, rest of masala and hot water. Add prunes, potatoes and carrots. Pile meat onto one side of saucepan, add prune mixture and cook, covered, over medium heat until vegetables are tender, adding a little more water if required. Serve with Gesmoorde ertjie rys (page 44).
SERVES 4.

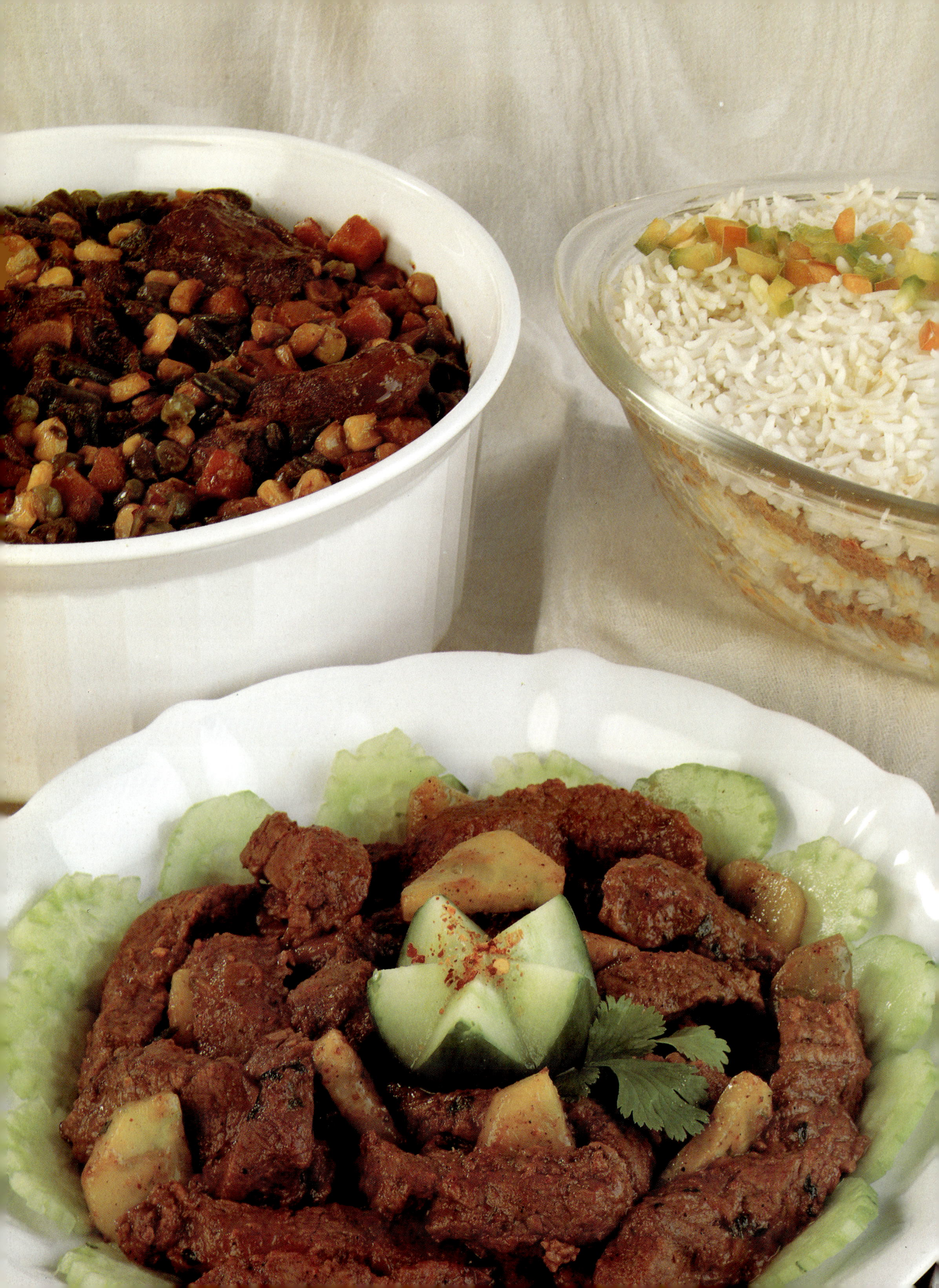

Clockwise from front left: Malaysian-style beef, Mutton and vegetable stew, Gheema mince pilau and Gheema curry with gem squash.

MUTTON AND LENTIL CURRY

*This **lang sous** (gravy) curry is very economical when catering for lots of holiday guests and family.*

375 ml brown lentils
20 ml cooking oil
2 onions, thinly sliced
500 g mutton or lamb, cubed
1 green chilli, finely chopped
10 ml crushed garlic
10 ml grated fresh root ginger
3 cardamom seeds
3 pieces stick cinnamon
5 ml borrie (turmeric)
10 ml red leaf masala
5 ml ground jeera (cumin)
5 ml ground koljander (coriander)
1 large tomato, skinned and grated
200 ml water
5 ml salt (or to taste)
5 ml sugar (optional)

Cover lentils with water and boil until soft, about 15–20 minutes. Rinse, drain and set aside until required. Meanwhile, heat oil in a large saucepan and fry onions until golden, 5–10 minutes. Add well-washed and drained meat and braise, covered, for 30 minutes. Add spices and tomato and cook, covered, for about 10 minutes. Add lentils and water and cook over moderate heat until well blended, about 20 minutes. Add salt and sugar to taste. Serve on a bed of white rice with atjars.
SERVES 6–8.

GHEEMA MINCE PILAU

Gheema mince pilau is best cooked in a clear glass casserole to show off the different layers of rice and mince – an attractive presentation at a formal dinner.

625 ml basmati rice
10 ml salt
5 whole cloves
2 pieces stick cinnamon
100 g butter, melted
2 onions, finely sliced
500 g lean mince meat
10 ml grated fresh root ginger
5 ml crushed garlic
5 ml chilli powder
10 ml ground koljander (coriander)
45 ml natural yoghurt
a few strands saffron
5 ml salt (or to taste)
chopped red and green peppers for garnishing

36 • MORE CAPE MALAY COOKING

Preheat oven to 150 °C. Boil rice in water with salt, cloves and stick cinnamon until nearly done. Rinse, drain and set aside. Heat butter in saucepan and fry onions until golden brown, 10–15 minutes. Add mince and rest of spices and cook, covered, until mince is browned. Add yoghurt and cook until it turns rich brown in colour. Soak saffron in water, drain and add to mince mixture. Stir in salt and remove from heat. Using a large casserole dish, layer the rice and mince (starting and ending with rice) until ingredients have been used up. Place, covered, in cool (300 °C) oven until rice is cooked, about 30 minutes. Garnish with chopped red and green peppers. Serve hot with vegetarian curries and sambals.
SERVES 6–8.

FRIKKADELS WITH TOMATO AND SPAGHETTI

TOMATO SAUCE
30 ml cooking oil
3 onions, thinly sliced
1 kg ripe tomatoes, skinned and grated
30 ml tomato paste
100 ml water
5 ml crushed, dried red chillies
10 ml crushed garlic
10 ml salt
60 ml sugar (or to taste)

FRIKKADELS
2 slices stale bread, soaked in water and moisture squeezed out
500 g steak mince
1 onion, grated
5 ml salt
5 ml white pepper
2,5 ml grated nutmeg
1 egg, lightly beaten

For the sauce, heat oil in a deep saucepan and braise onions until golden brown, about 10 minutes. Add tomatoes and tomato paste mixed with water, chillies and garlic and cook, covered, over medium heat until thick, about 30 minutes. Add salt and sugar and cook a further 5 minutes. Meanwhile, combine all the ingredients for frikkadels in a separate bowl. Shape into balls and add to sauce. Cook, covered, without stirring too much, until frikkadels are cooked. Serve on a bed of hot, cooked spaghetti.
SERVES 6–8.

OVEN FRIKKADELS

Traditionally served for a Sunday lunch, with leftovers kept and served on breadrolls for supper.

500 g steak or mutton mince
3 slices bread
1 onion, thinly sliced
10 ml crushed garlic
5 ml salt
5 ml coarsely ground black pepper
30 ml freshly chopped parsley
1 large egg
2,5 ml grated nutmeg

Preheat oven to 200 °C. Wash and drain mince well. Soak bread in water for about 5 minutes, then squeeze out all the moisture. In a large bowl, combine mince and bread with rest of ingredients and mix well. Shape into frikkadels and place on greased baking sheet. Bake for about 30 minutes. Serve with Almond yellow rice (page 81), gem squash and carrots.
SERVES 6.

GHEEMA CURRY WITH GEM SQUASH

*An unusual but tasty way of serving the traditional **gheema** (cubed steak) curry.*

30 ml cooking oil
2 large onions, very thinly sliced
5 cardamom pods
5 whole cloves
3 pieces stick cinnamon
1 kg beef or mutton, cubed, washed and drained
10 ml salt
10 ml crushed garlic
15 ml grated fresh root ginger
5 ml borrie (turmeric)
10 ml roasted masala
5 ml ground jeera (cumin)
5 ml ground koljander (coriander)
5 ml chilli powder
2,5 ml sugar
2 tomatoes, skinned and grated
3 large gem squash, peeled, seeded and cubed

Heat oil in large saucepan, add onions and sauté until transparent. Add cardamom pods, cloves, stick cinnamon and beef or mutton and braise for about 15 minutes. Add salt, garlic and ginger and cook a further 15 minutes. Mix in rest of spices and tomatoes and cook until well blended, about 15 minutes. Add squash and cook, covered, until soft, about 10 minutes. Serve with white rice or rotis.
SERVES 12.

SEEKH KEBABS

Another favourite Cape Malay dish introduced by pilgrims from Mecca. These can be bought at street cafés all around Mecca and Medina.

500 g lean mince meat
5 ml ground koljander (coriander)
5 ml ground jeera (cumin)
2,5 ml chilli powder
2,5 ml garam masala
5 ml salt
1 onion, finely grated and juice squeezed out
1 egg
10 ml crushed garlic
1 green chilli, finely chopped
30 ml cooking oil
slices of tomato, onion and lemon for garnishing

Combine mince with rest of ingredients, except cooking oil. Apply some oil to hands and skewers and press meat evenly and firmly onto skewers. Place kebabs on a greased baking sheet, brush with oil and grill gently. Turn kebabs often so that they brown evenly. When they are ready, gently slide them off skewers so that they do not break. Serve immediately with braised rice, and garnish with slices of tomato, onion and lemon.
SERVES 4–6.

Cook's tip
To prevent skewers from burning under the grill, first soak them in water for about 30 minutes.

LIVER KEBABS

*A modern dish of Indonesian origin, served in true Malay fashion with **gesmoorde rys** and chutney.*

1 kg lamb liver
juice of 2 lemons
10 ml chilli powder
salt to taste
butter and cooking oil for basting

Soak liver in cold water for about 15 minutes. Remove membrane and sinews, wash and dry and cut into 4 cm cubes. Marinate liver cubes in lemon juice, chilli powder and salt for about 1 hour. Thread liver onto skewers and grill gently, basting with butter and oil mixture and turning frequently until cooked through.
SERVES 6–8.

POOTJIES EN BOONTJIES

This is a favourite Cape Malay dish, traditionally served at funerals.

625 ml sugar beans, soaked overnight
1 ox trotter, well cleaned
30 ml cooking oil
2 large onions, thinly sliced
10 ml crushed garlic
5 ml salt (or to taste)
5 ml white pepper
5 ml crushed, dried red chillies
30 ml tomato paste
15 ml sugar (optional)

Drain sugar beans and cook in water to cover until fairly soft, about 1 hour. Meanwhile, cook ox trotter in water to cover until tender, about 3 hours. Drain well, reserving liquid. Heat oil in large, deep saucepan and braise onions until golden brown, about 15 minutes. Add garlic, salt, pepper and chillies and mix well. Add well-cooked trotter and a little of the reserved liquid and cook, covered, for about 10 minutes. Add sugar beans, stir in tomato paste, adding more of the reserved liquid if required. Cook, covered, over medium heat for about 15 minutes, stirring frequently. Stir in sugar if desired. Serve with white rice and atjars.
SERVES 10–12.

Cook's tip
Instead of cooking trotters for 3 hours, use a pressure cooker and cook at 100 kPa for about 1 hour.

FRIED KIDNEYS

This is a light supper to serve after a heavy lunch.

500 g lambs' or sheeps' kidneys
20 ml cooking oil
2 onions, finely chopped
5 ml freshly ground black pepper
5 ml crushed, dried red chillies
5 ml salt (or to taste)
5 ml crushed garlic
10 ml paprika
lemon juice and dhunia (coriander) leaves for garnishing

Remove membrane and hard core from kidneys, wash and drain and cut into cubes. Heat oil and sauté onions until transparent. Add kidneys and rest of ingredients and simmer gently until kidneys are tender, about 10–15 minutes, stirring frequently. Sprinkle with lemon juice and garnish with dhunia leaves. Serve with Mashed potatoes (page 83) or toast.
SERVES 10.

BOILED OX TONGUE

This versatile meat can be served hot or cold, and is ideal for filling sandwiches.

1 pickled ox tongue
5 whole cloves
3 whole allspice
5 bay leaves
5 pickling onions, peeled
1 litre water (or more if required)

Soak tongue in cold water to cover for about 30 minutes. Wash and scrape well with back of knife. Rinse well and drain. Combine tongue and rest of ingredients in a large, deep saucepan and bring to the boil, then reduce heat and simmer, covered, for about 3 hours or until tender. Slit underside of skin, peel it off and cut away the roots. Slice and serve hot with boiled vegetables or cold with fresh salads.
SERVES 8–10.

Cook's tip
If you find the ox tongue too hot to handle, plunge it in cold water for about 10 minutes so that the skin can come off more easily.

GARLIC ROAST OX TONGUE

For those who do not like the taste of garlic, it can be removed just before serving, or it can be omitted completely.

1 ox tongue
10 small cloves garlic
10 ml salt
10 ml freshly ground black pepper
50 ml cooking oil
5 whole cloves
3 whole allspice
3 bay leaves
250 ml hot water
10 baby potatoes

Soak tongue in boiling water to cover for about 30 minutes. Drain and scrape tongue very well with the back of a knife, then rinse in cold water. Make 10 small slits in tongue and insert a garlic clove in each slit. Sprinkle with salt and pepper, covering tongue completely. Heat oil in large, deep saucepan. Add tongue and spices and brown, about 10 minutes a side. Add hot water and steam, covered, over medium heat for about 1 hour or until tender. Add more water if necessary and turn tongue over from time to time. Add potatoes and cook for a further 10 minutes or until tender. Serve with boiled vegetables.
SERVES 10.

Front to back: Liver kebabs, Seekh kebabs and Fried kidneys with Mashed potatoes.

MEAT • 39

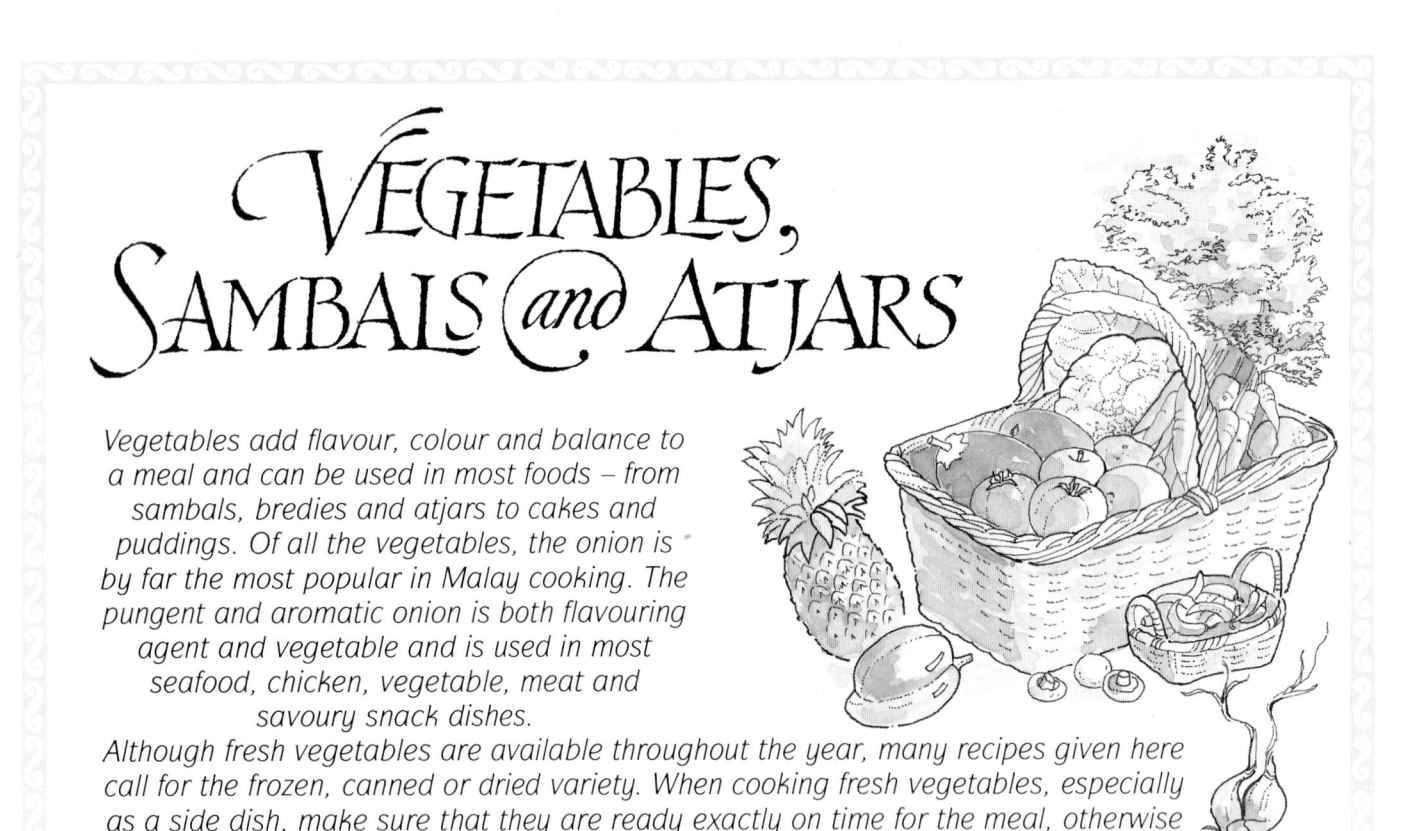

Vegetables, Sambals and Atjars

Vegetables add flavour, colour and balance to a meal and can be used in most foods – from sambals, bredies and atjars to cakes and puddings. Of all the vegetables, the onion is by far the most popular in Malay cooking. The pungent and aromatic onion is both flavouring agent and vegetable and is used in most seafood, chicken, vegetable, meat and savoury snack dishes.

Although fresh vegetables are available throughout the year, many recipes given here call for the frozen, canned or dried variety. When cooking fresh vegetables, especially as a side dish, make sure that they are ready exactly on time for the meal, otherwise they will lose flavour, colour and vitamins.

POTATO AND PEA CURRY

For a sweeter-tasting curry, use fresh peas if available instead of frozen peas.

45 ml cooking oil
1 onion, thinly sliced
500 g potatoes, peeled and cubed
5 ml chilli powder
2,5 ml borrie (turmeric)
5 ml ground koljander (coriander)
5 ml jeera (cumin) seeds
1 x 225 g can tomato purée
salt to taste
125 ml frozen peas
1 green pepper, seeded and sliced
200 ml water
chopped dhunia (coriander) leaves for garnishing

Heat oil in a large saucepan and braise onion until golden brown. Add potatoes and fry for 5 minutes. Stir in chilli powder, borrie, koljander and jeera and fry for about 2 minutes. Add tomatoes, salt, peas and green peppers and stir well. Cover and cook over moderate heat for about 2 minutes, then stir in the water. Cook until the potatoes are tender. Garnish with chopped dhunia leaves and serve with rotis or white rice.
SERVES 4.

DRY SPICY POTATO CURRY

This dry spicy curry makes a delicious light meal when served with Indian puris (page 84).

5 ml jeera (cumin) seeds
2,5 ml methi (fenugreek) seeds
5 ml chilli powder or 1 crushed, dried red chilli
1 onion, peeled and thinly sliced
30 ml cooking oil
450 g potatoes, peeled and cut into chunks
10 fresh curry leaves
5 ml mustard seeds
2,5 ml salt (or to taste)
2,5 ml borrie (turmeric)
15 ml desiccated coconut

In a frying pan dry-roast the jeera, methi and chilli powder or crushed, dried red chilli for about 1 minute. Add the onion and 10 ml oil and fry for 1 minute. Remove from heat and grind to a paste with a little water. Boil potatoes in lightly salted water until tender and drain well. Heat the remaining oil in a saucepan and add the curry leaves, mustard seeds and quick-fry for about 30 seconds. Add the paste, the potatoes, the rest of the ingredients and a little water and cook, covered, over low heat for about 5 minutes. Serve as a side dish with Pot-roast leg of lamb (page 79) or fried fish.
SERVES 4.

CAULIFLOWER CURRY

The lemon juice which is sprinkled over the cauliflower imparts a tangy flavour to this hot curry.

1 medium cauliflower
60 ml cooking oil
1 medium onion, finely chopped
5 ml jeera (cumin) seeds
2 potatoes, peeled and cut into chunks
5 ml chilli powder
2,5 ml borrie (turmeric)
10 ml ground koljander (coriander)
10 ml garam masala
30 ml fresh lemon juice

Break the cauliflower into florets and slice the remaining stem. Wash and soak in cold water for about 15 minutes, then drain well. Heat the oil in a deep saucepan and fry the onion until golden brown. Add the jeera seeds and the potatoes and fry for about 3 minutes. Stir in the cauliflower and fry for about 5 minutes. Add rest of ingredients, cover and cook gently for 10–15 minutes, or until potatoes and cauliflower are tender and the mixture is dry. Add a little water during cooking to prevent the mixture from sticking. Serve with rotis or white rice.
SERVES 4.

VARIATION
Five minutes before removing the curry from the heat, add 125 ml green peas.

OKRA CURRY

Okra, also known as ladies' fingers or gambo, has a flavour resembling that of baby marrows.

450 g okra
45 ml melted butter or cooking oil
1 onion, peeled and thinly sliced
225 g potatoes, peeled and cubed
5 ml chilli powder
7,5 ml ground koljander (coriander)
2,5 ml borrie (turmeric)
salt to taste

Wash, dry and cut off ends of the okra. Chop into 3 cm pieces. Heat the butter or oil in a saucepan and fry the onion until tender. Add the potatoes and fry for 3–5 minutes. Stir in the rest of the ingredients and cook, covered, over low heat for 10–15 minutes, or until the potatoes and okra are tender. If the mixture becomes too dry during cooking, add a little water. Serve with roti or white rice.
SERVES 4.

VARIATIONS
- **Baby marrow curry:** Use baby marrows instead of okra.
- Instead of okra, use 450 g cauliflower, butternut, green beans, or vegetable of choice.

Cook's tip
Okra has a gluey sap, and should therefore always be washed first, dried and then cut.

DRY CARROT AND POTATO CURRY

30 ml cooking oil
5 ml jeera (cumin) seeds
225 g carrots, diced
225 g potatoes, diced
5 ml chilli powder
5 ml borrie (turmeric)
5 ml ground koljander (coriander)
2,5 ml salt (or to taste)
120 ml water
30 ml chopped dhunia (coriander) leaves for garnishing

Heat the oil in a frying pan and fry the jeera seeds until they crackle. Add the carrots and potatoes and continue frying for about 5–6 minutes. Add the chilli powder, borrie, koljander, salt and water. Cook, covered, for about 5–10 minutes, or until the carrots and potatoes are tender and the mixture is dry. Garnish with dhunia leaves and serve on a bed of *gesmoorde rys*.
SERVES 4.

BRAISED BRINJALS WITH GARLIC

A very old traditional Malay way to serve brinjals.

450 g brinjals
45 ml cooking oil
2 potatoes, peeled and cut into chunks
5 cloves garlic, peeled and lightly crushed
2,5 ml chilli powder
2,5 ml borrie (turmeric)
7,5 ml ground koljander (coriander)
2,5 ml salt (or to taste)

Cut brinjals into cubes and soak in lightly salted water for about 10 minutes, then drain and pat dry. Heat the oil in a saucepan and fry the potatoes for 5–6 minutes. Add the garlic and continue frying until garlic is golden brown. Add brinjals and rest of ingredients and cook, covered, over low heat for about 10 minutes, or until the potatoes are tender. Do not stir too vigorously as the brinjals are very delicate. The garlic can be removed before serving.
SERVES 4.

VEGETABLE FRITTERS

Delicious as a snack, dipped in hot tomato chutney.

1 brinjal, sliced with skin on
2,5 ml salt
2 potatoes, peeled and sliced
2 onions, peeled and sliced
1 green pepper, sliced
250 ml cauliflower florets
cooking oil for deep-frying

BATTER
500 ml chana flour
5 ml baking powder
5 ml chilli powder
5 ml salt
juice of 1 lemon

Sprinkle brinjal with salt and set aside for about 10 minutes. Rinse under cold water and pat dry. Soak potatoes, onions, green pepper and cauliflower in cold water for approximately 10 minutes. Drain well and pat dry. Meanwhile, prepare batter by sifting together all the dry ingredients. Add sufficient water to make a thick batter, then add lemon juice and mix to combine well. Heat oil in a deep pan until a drop of the batter in the oil rises quickly and turns crisp. Dip the vegetables in the batter, a few at a time, and deep-fry until golden brown and crisp. Drain on paper towel and keep hot while frying the rest of the fritters.
SERVES 4–6.

MALAYSIAN STIR-FRY

This quick and easy stir-fry dish of Malaysian origin makes a lovely balanced meal as it contains chicken, prawns, noodles and a variety of vegetables.

300 g chicken breasts
300 g prawns, shelled and deveined
5 ml crushed, dried red chillies
5 cloves garlic
10 shallots
30 ml cooking oil
3 eggs
1 x 1 kg packet noodles, cooked
500 g cabbage, finely shredded
500 g bean sprouts
500 g spring onions, cut into 3 cm pieces
3 tomatoes, sliced
30 ml soy sauce
salt to taste
pinch of sugar (optional)
3 stalks celery, chopped for garnishing
1 small onion, thinly sliced

Skin and bone chicken and cut into strips. Wash and drain well. Wash prawns and drain well. Pound together chillies, garlic and shallots. Heat oil in wok or deep frying pan and fry pounded ingredients until the aroma comes out. Add chicken strips and fry, uncovered, for 5 minutes. Add eggs, prawns and noodles and cook a further 5 minutes. Stir in rest of ingredients and stir-fry until all the vegetables are cooked but still crisp. Garnish with celery and serve hot.
SERVES 8.

DRY SPICY CORN

Dry spicy corn is a delicious filling for gem squash.

45 ml cooking oil or butter
1 small onion, thinly sliced
5–6 curry leaves
1 x 410 g can whole kernel corn
½ green pepper, diced (optional)
5 ml ground koljander (coriander)
2,5 ml borrie (turmeric)
15 ml chopped dhunia (coriander) leaves
salt to taste

Heat oil in saucepan and sauté onion until transparent. Add curry leaves and cook a further 2 minutes. Add drained corn, green pepper, koljander and borrie and cook, covered, until all excess liquid has evaporated, about 5 minutes. Add chopped dhunia leaves and salt and cook, uncovered, for about 1 minute. Serve as a side dish.
SERVES 4.

SWEETCORN LAGAN

This casserole of Indian origin makes a lovely vegetarian meal if served with Vegetable soup (page 27) as a starter.

200 ml self-raising flour
5 ml salt
1 ml white pepper
2,5 ml borrie (turmeric)
2,5 ml ground jeera (cumin)
2,5 ml ground koljander (coriander)
2,5 ml crushed, dried red chillies
½ bunch chopped dhunia (coriander) leaves
1 green chilli, finely chopped
1 x 410 g can cream-style sweetcorn
3 eggs, well beaten
30 ml soft butter

Preheat oven to 180 °C. Sift all dry ingredients together. Add rest of ingredients and mix well. Pour mixture into a well-greased casserole dish and bake until set, about 30 minutes.
SERVES 6 AS A SIDE DISH AND 4 AS A MAIN COURSE.

42 • *MORE CAPE MALAY COOKING*

Clockwise from back: Baby marrow curry, Vegetable fritters and Carrot and apple atjar.

VEGETABLES, SAMBALS AND ATJARS

GESMOORDE ERTJIE RYS

A perfect accompaniment to curries, breyanis and bredies.

500 ml basmati rice
30 ml soft butter
30 ml cooking oil
1 onion, thinly sliced
2 pieces stick cinnamon
3 cardamom pods
2 whole cloves
½ green pepper, seeded and diced
125 ml frozen green peas
5 ml crushed, dried red chillies

Wash rice until water runs clear. Boil in lightly salted water until tender, then rinse and drain well. Heat butter and oil in a deep saucepan and braise onion until golden and crisp, about 10–15 minutes. Add spices and cook for another 2 minutes. Add green pepper and peas and cook for about 10 minutes. Add drained rice and chillies and combine well. Steam, covered, over low heat for 20–30 minutes.
SERVES 6–8.

Cook's tip
Combine ingredients as above in a casserole dish, then cook, covered, in oven at 180 °C for 15 minutes, or in microwave on 50% for 8–10 minutes.

DHAL SAUCE WITH BRAISED ONION

A delicious red lentil sauce, garnished with onion.

300 ml dhal (red lentils)
2,5 ml borrie (turmeric)
10 ml ground koljander (coriander)
1 green chilli, halved and seeded
2 tomatoes, skinned and grated or
1 x 225 g can tomato purée
salt to taste
6 curry leaves
45 ml butter
1 small onion, thinly sliced

Boil lentils in water with borrie and koljander until soft, about 15–20 minutes. Drain lentils and mash to get a smoother texture. Stir in green chilli, tomatoes, salt and curry leaves. Cook, covered, over low heat for about 20 minutes. Remove from heat and set aside. In a separate saucepan, heat butter and fry onion until light brown and slightly crisp. Garnish the dhal sauce with fried onion and serve on a bed of white rice as an accompaniment to Dry spicy masala fish (page 24).
SERVES 6.

BRAISED TURNIPS

500 g turnips, peeled
100 ml hot water
75 ml soft butter
1 onion, peeled and thinly sliced
1 green chilli, finely chopped
5 ml garam masala
2,5 ml salt (or to taste)
5 ml sugar (optional)
15 ml fresh lemon juice

Slice the turnips into rounds, then wash and drain. Cook the turnips in the hot water until tender and dry. Heat the butter in a saucepan and fry onion until golden brown. Add the turnips and remaining ingredients, except lemon juice, and cook for a further 5 minutes. Sprinkle with lemon juice and serve as a side dish.
SERVES 4.

APPLE, QUINCE AND PINEAPPLE SAMBAL

This delicious and fresh-tasting combination makes a fruity sambal which goes well with curries or bredies.

3 large Granny Smith apples
1 large quince
5 ml salt
1 medium pineapple
5 ml crushed garlic
2 green chillies, finely chopped
30 ml sugar
50 ml white vinegar
100 ml chopped dhunia (coriander) leaves

Peel and coarsely grate apples and quince. Sprinkle with salt and allow to draw for 15 minutes, then drain off all the moisture. Peel and grate pineapple. Combine all ingredients in a salad bowl and serve.
SERVES 6.

CUCUMBER, ONION AND CELERY SAMBAL

A fresh-tasting combination, ideal to serve with any curry or breyani dish.

1 large cucumber, peeled and sliced
1 large onion, thinly sliced and blanched
3 stalks table celery, finely chopped
30 ml chilli sauce or tomato chutney

Arrange cucumber and onion rings in a bowl. Sprinkle chopped celery over and refrigerate until required. Before serving, pour the chilli sauce or tomato chutney over the cucumber and onion rings.
SERVES 6.

CUCUMBER AND PINEAPPLE SAMBAL

A tangy and cool sambal, which is the ideal accompaniment to any curry or breyani dish.

1 large English cucumber, peeled and sliced
250 ml fresh pineapple cubes
1 small onion, grated
1 small green chilli, finely chopped
pinch of salt
½ green pepper, sliced (optional)

Mix together all ingredients and chill. Transfer sambal to a salad bowl and serve.
SERVES 8–10.

CARROT AND APPLE ATJAR

This quick and easy atjar can be served immediately, unlike other atjars which need to mature.

5 carrots
3 large Granny Smith apples
5 ml salt
250 ml cooking oil
50 ml atjar masala

Peel and coarsely grate carrots and apples. Sprinkle with salt and allow to draw for 15 minutes. Drain off moisture. Mix 30 ml cooking oil and atjar masala together. Heat remaining oil and add to masala paste. Combine carrots, apples and masala and mix to blend well. Set aside to cool, then bottle in sterilized jars and seal.
MAKES ABOUT 500 ml.

EASY LEMON ATJAR

1 kg fresh lemons
75 ml salt
750 ml white vinegar
150 ml cooking oil
25 ml chilli powder
5 ml crushed koljander (coriander) seeds
5 ml crushed jeera (cumin) seeds
100 ml methi masala
65 ml sugar
5 ml mustard powder

Wash lemons well and dry. Cut each into eighths and remove pips. Dissolve salt in vinegar and soak lemons in it for 48 hours, stirring frequently to ensure that all the lemons are well soaked. Pour off excess liquid. Add rest of ingredients and mix well. Bottle in sterilized jars and seal. Set aside for 24 hours before using.
MAKES 1 kg.

STUFFED GREEN CHILLI ATJAR

A hot, but delicious, atjar which can also be served on cold meat sandwiches.

24 large green chillies
30 ml cooking oil for shallow-frying

MASALA STUFFING
30 ml crushed garlic
5 ml salt
10 ml borrie (turmeric)
10 ml red leaf masala
10 ml cooking oil

Wash chillies, keeping stems intact, then slit lengthwise without cutting through. Combine stuffing ingredients and mix to a thick paste. Stuff chillies with prepared stuffing. Heat oil in frying pan and stir-fry stuffed chillies for about 5 minutes. (At this stage, the filling will start oozing out, making a thick sauce.) Serve with masala steak, potato chips and savoury rice.
MAKES 24 STUFFED CHILLIES.

Front: Doughnuts sprinkled with icing sugar. Back: Quick ring doughnuts with glacé icing and nuts.

BREADS and PIZZAS

Bread, in all its forms, is a universal staple food, most countries having developed their own variety. Although many Cape Malays still prefer rotis, rice or puris with their curries, bread and rolls too are becoming everyday fare for them. A great variety of delicious breads and rolls are given here, ranging from pizza and savoury bread to fruit-filled and spicy ones. Because of the trend towards more wholesome foods, I have included bran muffins and wholewheat breads too. As with many other international dishes, Malays have adapted pizzas to suit their tastes, with toppings such as savoury mince and mixed vegetables.

MALAY ROTIS

*A **roti** is unleavened bread made from flour, and is served instead of rice, with chutney. A roti rolled around Curry mince filling (page 13) is known as a **salomi** – a traditional Malay fast food.*

750 ml cake flour
100 ml self-raising flour
5 ml salt
45 ml cooking oil or softened butter
250 ml cold water
100 ml cake flour
90 g butter
50 ml melted butter mixed with 50 ml cooking oil

Combine flours and salt in a bowl. Add oil or butter, rubbing it into flour to form a crumbly mixture. Add water and mix to a soft dough. Knead, adding more flour (if required) to make an even-textured, pliable dough. Leave, covered, to rest for 30 minutes. Divide dough into 7-8 pieces. Roll each out on a very lightly floured surface to a circle 20 cm in diameter, dot with 15 ml butter and sprinkle with flour. Roll and stretch into thick ropes of dough (Fig. 1). Roll up both ends of the ropes; one side clockwise, one anti-clockwise (Fig. 2), and fold one half flat on top of the other (Fig. 3). (Rotis may be frozen at this stage, interleaved with plastic.) Allow to rest, covered, for about 1 hour. Roll out on a lightly floured surface to circles about 20 cm in diameter. Heat a heavy-based frying pan and fry rotis one at a time, turning occasionally and brushing with melted butter and oil mixture (about 10 ml in all for each one). Fry until golden. Remove from pan and pat between palms to fluff surface.

MAKES 7-8.

Microwave tip
To reheat rotis, cover and microwave on 50% for 20-30 seconds per roti.

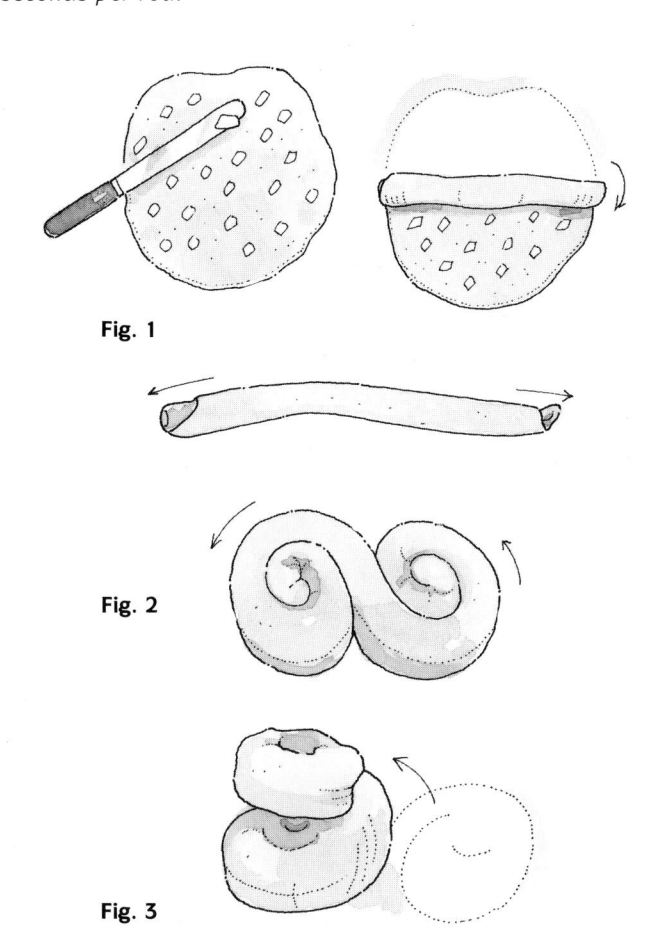

Fig. 1

Fig. 2

Fig. 3

QUICK-AND-EASY PIZZA

For snack-sized pizzas, roll out dough, cut into 7 cm circles and proceed as below.

BASE
500 ml self-raising flour
500 ml cake flour
5 ml salt
30 ml cooking oil
500 ml natural yoghurt
chutney (or peri-peri) and tomato sauce for spreading

Preheat oven to 200 °C. Sift flours and salt in a bowl. Add oil and mix until mixture resembles breadcrumbs. Gradually add yoghurt to make a soft, slightly sticky dough. With oiled hands, pat dough into two large, round pizza or Swiss roll pans. Raise edges slightly. Bake on middle shelf of oven for about 10 minutes or until light gold. Spread with sauce made up of equal quantities of chutney or peri-peri sauce and tomato sauce. Top with topping of your choice. Return to oven and bake for a further 10 minutes.
MAKES 2 PIZZA BASES.

TOPPINGS

- Top with Mince filling (page 12), slices of tomato and green pepper and grated cheese.
- Top with lightly steamed sausages, slices of tomato and green pepper and grated cheese.
- Instead of the chutney and tomato sauce, combine 250 ml tomato purée, 10 ml brown sugar and 10 ml mixed herbs and spread over pizza bases. Heat 15 ml cooking oil in a frying pan and stir-fry 500 ml mixed and diced vegetables. Top pizza base with a layer of grated cheese, vegetables and another layer of grated cheese.

QUICK RING DOUGHNUTS

One of the favourites for sending to neighbours and friends during Ramadan.

500 ml cake flour
2,5 ml bicarbonate of soda
5 ml cream of tartar
1 ml ground cinnamon
60 ml soft butter
60 ml castor sugar
1 egg, beaten
milk for mixing
cooking oil for deep-frying
chopped nuts for garnishing

GLACÉ ICING
125 ml icing sugar, sifted
20 ml water

Sift together flour, bicarbonate of soda, cream of tartar and cinnamon into a large bowl and rub in butter with fingertips. Stir in sugar and mix well. Make a well in centre, pour in egg and work it into the mixture to form a stiff dough, adding milk if necessary. Turn onto a floured surface and knead quickly and lightly to remove cracks. Roll out on a floured surface to about 2 cm thick. Using a floured doughnut cutter, cut out rings as close to each other as possible. Heat oil in deep saucepan and fry doughnuts (a few at a time) until light golden brown, turning them frequently. Lift out with a slotted spoon and drain on paper towel. The centres cut from the doughnuts can be fried as well. Mix icing ingredients to a smooth paste. Spread over doughnuts and sprinkle with nuts.
MAKES ABOUT 20 RING DOUGHNUTS AND 20 SMALL BALLS.

VARIATION
Omit the glacé icing and sprinkle with castor or icing sugar.

LEMON FRUIT PLAIT

A very easy and attractive sweet loaf to serve on Sunday mornings instead of the traditional koesisters.

560 ml self-raising flour
60 g butter or margarine
20 ml castor sugar
50 ml sultanas
10 ml grated lemon rind
1 egg, lightly beaten
125 ml milk
30 ml mixed peel
30 ml chopped glacé cherries

SUGAR GLACÉ
15 ml sugar
30 ml hot water

LEMON ICING
200 ml sifted icing sugar
15 ml lemon juice
15 ml soft butter
±15 ml boiling water

Preheat oven to 180 °C. Sift flour into a bowl and rub in butter or margarine until it resembles breadcrumbs. Stir in sugar, sultanas and lemon rind, then egg and enough milk to mix to a soft pliable dough. Knead on lightly floured surface until smooth. Divide dough into three pieces. Roll each piece into a rope about 30 cm long. Plait the ropes firmly together. Place on well-greased baking sheet and tuck ends in underneath. Bake for about 20 minutes. Combine sugar glacé ingredients and brush over fruit plait. Return to oven and bake a further 5 minutes. Lift onto wire rack to cool. Meanwhile, for icing, sift icing sugar into bowl, stir in lemon juice, butter and enough water to mix to a pouring consistency. Pour over cake and sprinkle with mixed peel and cherries.
MAKES 1 FRUIT PLAIT.

FLOP-PROOF BANANA LOAF

An unusually soft loaf to serve with tea or for breakfast. Banana loaf improves its flavour when stored in an airtight container for a day or two.

125 g butter or margarine
250 ml sugar
3 bananas, peeled and mashed
2 eggs
500 ml cake flour
pinch of salt
5 ml bicarbonate of soda
65 ml water
7,5 ml baking powder

Preheat oven to 180 °C. Cream butter or margarine and sugar until light and creamy. Stir in mashed bananas and beat to combine thoroughly. Beat in eggs one at a time, stirring to combine well. Sift in flour and salt and mix. Dissolve bicarbonate of soda in water and stir into mixture. Add baking powder and mix. Pour batter into a greased and lined loaf pan and bake for about 45 minutes. Allow to cool in the pan for about 10 minutes before turning out onto a wire rack. Serve sliced and buttered.
MAKES 1 LOAF.

SAVOURY CHEESE LOAF

Ideal to serve at a braai or when entertaining guests. The buttermilk gives it a good lasting quality.

4 x 250 ml self-raising flour
5 ml salt
5 ml baking powder
500 ml buttermilk
1 egg, lightly beaten
250 ml grated Cheddar cheese
10 ml dried mixed herbs
1 very small grated onion, juice squeezed out

Preheat oven to 180 °C. Sift together flour, salt and baking powder into a bowl. Combine buttermilk and egg and beat thoroughly. Add grated cheese, mixed herbs and onion. Stir buttermilk and egg mixture into dry ingredients and blend well. Pour dough into a well-greased and lined loaf pan and bake for about 1 hour. Turn out onto wire rack and remove paper from base.
MAKES 1 LOAF.

WHOLEWHEAT LOAF

750 ml wholewheat flour
250 ml cake flour
100 ml crushed wheat
7,5 ml instant dried yeast
5 ml salt
100 ml sunflower seeds
25 ml cooking oil
25 ml honey or golden syrup
±450 ml warm water
sunflower seeds for topping

Grease and line a 23 cm x 9 cm loaf pan. Mix flours, crushed wheat, yeast, salt and sunflower seeds in a bowl. Mix in oil and honey. Add 300 ml of the water, then stir in just enough of the remaining water to make a soft, sticky dough. Mix well, then turn into pan. Sprinkle with sunflower seeds, pressing lightly into the dough. Cover dough with a damp cloth and leave to rise in a warm place until about 2 cm over the top of pan. Bake at 200 °C on middle shelf of oven for 30 minutes and then at 180 °C for a further 30 minutes. Turn out onto wire rack and leave to cool.
MAKES 1 MEDIUM-SIZED LOAF.

INSTANT WHOLEWHEAT BREAD

A quick and easy bread to prepare.

4 x 250 ml wholewheat flour
5 ml salt
5 ml bicarbonate of soda
20 ml cooking oil
15 ml honey, golden syrup or brown sugar
100 ml seedless raisins or sultanas
500 ml buttermilk
50 ml sunflower seeds
sunflower seeds for topping

Preheat oven to 180 °C. Grease and line a 23 cm x 9 cm loaf pan. Mix flour and salt in a bowl. Sift in bicarbonate of soda and mix well. Mix in oil, honey and raisins. Pour in buttermilk and stir with a wooden spoon until ingredients are thoroughly combined – the batter should be soft and sticky. Pour batter into prepared pan, sprinkle with sunflower seeds and bake on middle shelf of oven for about 1 hour. Remove from pan and allow to stand for about 5 minutes, then return loaf to oven on a baking sheet to crisp the sides. Cool on wire rack.
MAKES 1 MEDIUM-SIZED LOAF.

BREADS AND PIZZAS • 49

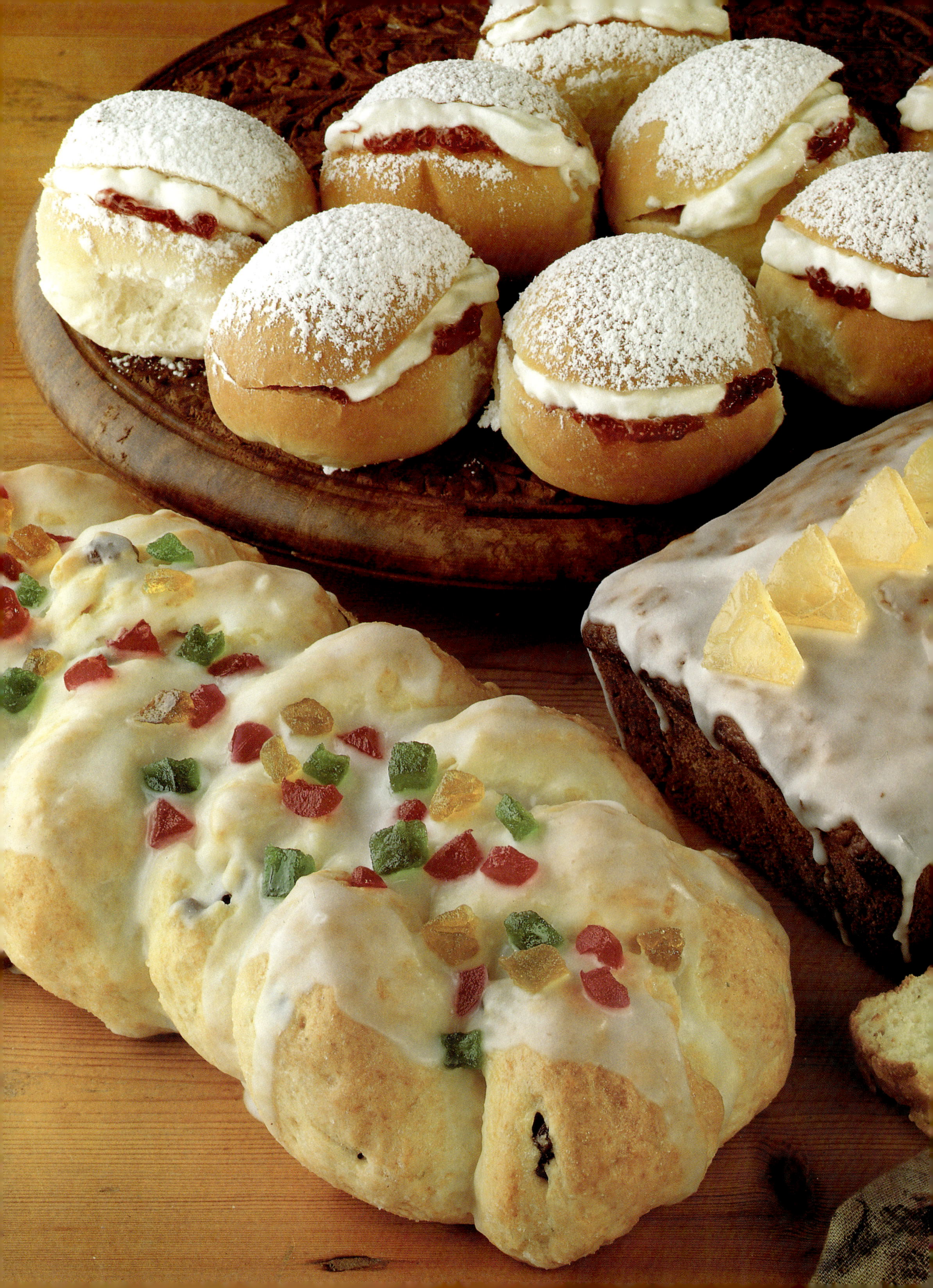

Clockwise from left: Lemon fruit plait, Soft milk buns, Pineapple tea bread and Savoury cheese loaf.

SPICY FRUIT BUNS

These delicious buns can also be served sliced and buttered for breakfast.

4 x 250 ml cake flour
5 ml mixed spice
2,5 ml ground cinnamon
5 ml salt
60 g butter or margarine
60 ml currants or sultanas
60 ml chopped mixed peel
125 ml castor sugar
10 ml active dried yeast
125 ml lukewarm milk
125 ml lukewarm water
1 egg, lightly beaten

Sift flour, mixed spice, cinnamon and salt into a bowl. Rub in butter or margarine, then mix in currants or sultanas, mixed peel and 115 ml castor sugar. Dissolve yeast in lukewarm milk and water mixture to which reserved castor sugar has been added. Leave for about 15 minutes or until frothy. Add yeast mixture and egg to flour and mix to form a soft dough. Turn dough out onto a lightly floured surface and knead until smooth and elastic. Shape into a ball and place in a lightly greased bowl, turning dough over so that top of dough is also greased. Cover with a damp cloth and leave to rise in a warm place until doubled in size, about 1½ hours. Turn dough out onto a lightly floured surface. Divide into 16 pieces and shape each into a small ball. Place balls far apart on a greased baking sheet to allow for spreading. Cover with a damp cloth and leave to rise for about 30 minutes. Bake at 200 °C on middle shelf of oven for about 15 minutes. Turn out onto wire rack and leave to cool. Spread with Glacé icing (page 48).
MAKES 16.

PINEAPPLE TEA BREAD

750 ml self-raising flour
2,5 ml salt
65 ml butter or margarine
125 ml castor sugar
1 large egg, beaten
1 x 440 g can crushed pineapple
100 ml evaporated milk

Preheat oven to 190 °C. Sift flour and salt into a bowl and rub in butter or margarine until mixture resembles breadcrumbs. Stir in castor sugar and beaten egg. Mix in pineapple and juice. Add evaporated milk and mix well. Pour into greased and lined loaf pan and bake for about 1½ hours. Turn out onto wire rack to cool and remove paper. Serve warm, topped with Glacé icing (page 48).
MAKES 1 LOAF.

PUMPKIN BOLLAS

A traditional Cape Malay favourite served at Ramadan. It is also an ideal way of using up leftover pumpkin.

30 ml soft butter
500 g pumpkin, cooked
4 x 250 ml self-raising flour, sifted
2,5 ml salt
10 ml baking powder
60 ml sugar
2 eggs, lightly beaten
5 ml vanilla essence
milk to mix
cooking oil for deep-frying

CINNAMON SUGAR
250 ml castor sugar
10 ml ground cinnamon

Mash butter into hot pumpkin. Sift all the dry ingredients together into a large bowl. Mix in pumpkin and rest of ingredients, adding a little milk to make a thick batter. Drop spoonfuls into moderately hot oil and deep-fry until golden brown. Remove with a slotted spoon and drain on paper towel. Mix ingredients for cinnamon sugar and use to coat bollas.
MAKES ABOUT 45.

BUTTERMILK SCONES

These soft, long-lasting scones are ideal to serve for breakfast or at a picnic.

4 x 250 ml self-raising flour, sifted
5 ml salt
60 ml castor sugar
125 g butter or margarine
1 extra-large egg
250 ml buttermilk
beaten egg for brushing (optional)

Preheat oven to 200 °C. Sift flour, salt and castor sugar together. Rub in butter or margarine until mixture resembles breadcrumbs. Beat egg into buttermilk. Add buttermilk mixture to dry ingredients and mix to a very soft dough. Turn dough out onto floured surface and roll out to 2 cm thick. Cut out rounds with biscuit cutter. Place scones on greased baking sheets and brush with egg. Bake on middle shelf of oven for 15-20 minutes or until golden brown on top.
MAKES ABOUT 24 SCONES.

VARIATIONS
♦ Omit castor sugar and add 125 ml chopped dates.
♦ Add 125 ml seedless raisins, sultanas or currants.

PIESANG KOLWYNTJIES

125 g margarine
250 ml castor sugar
2 eggs
5 ml vanilla essence
4 ripe bananas, mashed
500 ml cake flour, sifted
5 ml baking powder
5 ml bicarbonate of soda
125 ml hot water

Preheat oven to 180 °C. Cream margarine and sugar until light and creamy. Add eggs one at a time, beating well after each addition. Stir in vanilla essence and mashed bananas. Add flour and baking powder, followed by bicarbonate of soda dissolved in hot water. Mix until well combined. Spoon into greased muffin pans and bake for 20-25 minutes. Allow to cool before turning out onto wire racks.
MAKES ABOUT 24.

VARIATIONS
- Add 175 ml chopped, mixed nuts, walnuts or pecan nuts to the muffin mixture.
- Add 75 ml seedless raisins, currants or sultanas to the muffin mixture.
- Add 5 ml ground mixed spice to the muffin mixture.

BRAN MUFFINS

A wholesome treat which can be adapted to suit slimmers by using 30 ml sweetener instead of the sugar.

625 ml wholewheat flour
500 ml digestive bran
15 ml bicarbonate of soda
60 ml brown sugar
2,5 ml salt
2 eggs, lightly beaten
90 ml cooking oil
250 ml milk
250 ml water
250 ml seedless raisins

Preheat oven to 180 °C. In a large bowl, combine all the dry ingredients and mix well. Make a well in the centre and mix in eggs, oil, milk and water. Add raisins and mix to a soft batter. Drop spoonfuls into greased muffin pans, about two-thirds full. Bake on middle shelf of oven for about 15 minutes. Cool on wire racks.
MAKES ABOUT 30.

VARIATIONS
- Add 250 ml cake fruit mix instead of raisins.
- Add 250 ml chopped dates instead of raisins.

SOFT MILK BUNS

These buns, if stored in an airtight container, will keep for up to three days.

4 x 250 ml cake flour, sifted
20 ml castor sugar
10 ml active dried yeast
125 ml warm milk
125 ml warm water
5 ml salt
65 g butter

Mix 250 ml cake flour with 5 ml sugar, yeast, milk and water and set aside until frothy, about 20-30 minutes. Mix remaining flour and salt. Add remaining sugar and rub in butter. Stir in yeast mixture and mix to a soft dough. Turn dough out onto a board and knead until smooth. Put in a greased bowl, cover with a damp cloth and leave at room temperature for about 1½ hours. Turn dough out onto board, divide into 15 pieces and shape into buns. Do not overwork the dough. A little oil on the palm of the hand helps to give a smooth finish. Place the buns far apart on a lightly floured baking sheet. Cover lightly with plastic and leave to rise until dough feels springy, about 30 minutes. Remove plastic and bake at 180 °C for 15-20 minutes. Cool on wire rack.
MAKES 15 BUNS.

VARIATION
These buns can be split diagonally, spread with strawberry or raspberry jam and piped with whipped fresh cream.

BREAKFAST CAKES

These flapjacks can easily be prepared by children, and also make delicious treats if served hot with honey or syrup, topped with whipped fresh cream.

1 egg, lightly beaten
30 ml sugar
125 ml milk
15 ml melted butter
250 ml cake flour
10 ml baking powder
1 ml salt
2,5 ml vanilla essence (optional)

Beat eggs and sugar together and add milk and melted butter. Sift flour, baking powder and salt and fold into egg mixture. Stir well to form a smooth batter. Add vanilla essence and mix well. Drop spoonfuls on a hot griddle or into a heavy-based frying-pan and fry on both sides. Serve hot, with honey, caramel syrup or jam.
MAKES ABOUT 15.

Front: Gingernut scraps. Back: Peppermint fingers.

Biscuits and Pastries

Biscuits and pastries are firm favourites in most Cape Malay homes, and included in this section are a variety to suit all palates. Nuts and desiccated coconut are popular ingredients in Malay baking, and are used extensively in the baking of biscuits. Although the recipes in this section are not all traditional Cape Malay ones, they have been adopted by the Malay community and are sometimes presented to neighbours during Ramadan, or are included in an engagement **barakat**. *This gift, beautifully wrapped in cellophane, is usually presented by the bride-to-be to her future husband's relatives after the couple have decided to marry.*
When baking biscuits, accurate measurement of ingredients and minimum handling of the dough is required. Biscuits also need careful watching while they are baking in the oven, as they burn very easily.

PEPPERMINT FINGERS

125 g butter
125 ml sugar
250 ml desiccated coconut
250 ml cake flour, sifted
15 ml cocoa powder
2,5 ml peppermint essence
5 ml baking powder
250 ml cornflakes, lightly crushed

ICING
90 g butter
160 ml icing sugar, sifted
1 ml peppermint essence
2 small bars Peppermint Crisp for decoration

Preheat oven to 180 °C. Cream butter and sugar. Beat in coconut, flour, cocoa, peppermint essence and baking powder and mix to blend well. Stir in cornflakes. Press dough about 1 cm thick into a lightly greased 25 cm x 30 cm Swiss roll pan. Bake for about 15–20 minutes, then cool on wire rack. For the icing, cream butter until light and gradually beat in icing sugar. Flavour with peppermint essence. Spread biscuits roughly with icing and sprinkle grated Peppermint Crisp over. Cut into finger biscuits.
MAKES ABOUT 50.

GINGERNUT SCRAPS

The cinnamon and ginger impart a delicious spicy flavour to these biscuits.

500 ml cake flour
250 ml castor sugar
2,5 ml bicarbonate of soda
5 ml ground cinnamon
pinch of salt
10 ml ground ginger
125 g butter
1 small egg
15 ml golden syrup

Preheat oven to 160 °C. Sift together flour, sugar, soda, cinnamon, salt and ginger and mix well. Rub in butter until mixture has a very fine crumbly consistency. Beat egg and golden syrup together and add to dry ingredients. Knead into a firm dough. Roll teaspoonfuls of mixture into small balls and place on lightly greased baking sheets, approximately 5 cm apart. Bake for about 15 minutes. Loosen biscuits and cool on wire racks.
MAKES ABOUT 40.

VARIATION
Place an almond flake on top of each biscuit before baking.

MELTING MOMENTS

These biscuits can be filled with lemon or orange cream.

250 g butter
90 ml icing sugar
375 ml cake flour
125 ml cornflour

LEMON CREAM
60 g butter
125 ml icing sugar, sifted
5 ml grated lemon rind
15 ml freshly squeezed lemon juice

Preheat oven to 180 °C. Cream butter and icing sugar until light and fluffy. Add sifted flour and cornflour and mix well. Put mixture into a piping bag fitted with a fluted tube. Pipe rosettes onto lightly greased baking sheets and bake for 10–12 minutes or until pale golden brown. Cool on wire racks. Meanwhile, for lemon cream, beat butter until smooth, gradually add icing sugar and beat until mixture is light and creamy. Beat in lemon rind and juice. Sandwich cooled biscuits together with lemon cream.
MAKES ABOUT 30 COMPLETE BISCUITS.

VARIATION
Orange cream: Substitute orange rind and juice for lemon rind and juice.

DATE AND COCONUT BISCUITS

250 g butter
60 ml cooking oil
250 ml sugar
2 eggs
5 ml vanilla essence
3 drops egg-yellow food colouring
4 x 250 ml cake flour, sifted
5 ml baking powder
1 x 250 g packet pitted dates, chopped
250 ml desiccated coconut
quartered glacé cherries for decoration

Preheat oven to 200 °C. Cream butter, oil and sugar until light and fluffy. Add eggs, vanilla essence and colouring, beating well after each addition. Add sifted flour and baking powder and blend well. Mix in dates and coconut to form a soft dough. Roll out to a thickness of about 3 mm on a lightly floured surface and scrape top with a fork to give a rough texture. Cut out rounds about 4 cm in diameter and place on a lightly greased baking sheet. Top each biscuit with a quartered cherry. Bake for about 10 minutes or until biscuits are light brown in colour.
MAKES ABOUT 80.

CHOCOLATE CHIP COOKIES

These Western delights are delicious with walnuts added as a variation.

125 g butter
125 ml white sugar
125 ml brown sugar, lightly packed
2,5 ml vanilla essence
1 egg, lightly beaten
440 ml self-raising flour
2,5 ml salt
125 g chocolate chips

Preheat oven to 180 °C. Cream together butter, sugars and vanilla essence. Fold in egg and add sifted flour and salt. Stir in chocolate chips and mix well. Shape teaspoonfuls of mixture into small balls, place on lightly greased baking sheet, allowing about 2 cm between each biscuit for spreading. Bake for about 12 minutes.
MAKES ABOUT 48.

CHOCOLATE DROPS

A delicious and fancy biscuit which is usually included in an engagement barakat.

100 g butter
200 ml castor sugar
50 g plain chocolate, melted
1 egg, beaten
5 ml vanilla essence
400 ml cake flour
2,5 ml salt
2,5 ml bicarbonate of soda
30 ml milk

ICING
50 g butter
50 g plain chocolate, melted
340 ml icing sugar
a few drops vanilla essence
halved pecan nuts or walnuts for decoration

Preheat oven to 200 °C. Cream butter, sugar and chocolate until fluffy. Beat in egg and vanilla essence. Add remaining ingredients for the biscuit mixture and stir until well blended. Drop teaspoonfuls of the mixture about 2,5 cm apart onto a lightly greased baking sheet. Bake for about 15 minutes or until biscuits are slightly puffy. Remove from baking sheet and cool on wire rack. For the icing, cream butter and melted chocolate. Gradually beat in sifted icing sugar until the mixture is smooth and creamy. Decorate each biscuit with a little icing and half a nut.
MAKES ABOUT 36.

PECAN NUT SCRAPS

300 ml pecan nuts
60 g butter
65 ml icing sugar
5 ml vanilla essence
125 ml cake flour

Preheat oven to 180 °C. Finely chop about a quarter of the nuts and reserve the rest. Cream butter, sifted icing sugar and vanilla essence until light and fluffy. Add chopped pecan nuts and stir in sifted flour. Use floured hands to form teaspoonfuls of mixture into balls. Place balls about 2 cm apart on lightly greased baking sheets. Press a pecan nut onto each ball, making a slight indentation. Bake for about 10 minutes or until golden brown. Cool on baking sheets and dust with sifted icing sugar before serving.
MAKES ABOUT 30.

COCONUT AND ALMOND SCRAPS

A traditional coconut biscuit with an almond taste.

200 ml sugar
250 g butter
30 ml cooking oil
250 ml chopped almonds, with skins on
250 ml desiccated coconut
500 ml cake flour, sifted
5 drops almond essence
quartered glacé cherries for decoration

Preheat oven to 200 °C. Cream sugar, butter and oil until light and creamy. Add remaining ingredients and mix to a soft dough. Roll out on a lightly floured surface to a thickness of 3 mm and scrape top with a fork to give a rough texture. Cut out rounds with a biscuit cutter and place on a lightly greased baking sheet. Place a quarter cherry on each biscuit, making a slight indentation. Bake for about 10 minutes or until golden brown in colour.
MAKES ABOUT 60.

AFGHAN BISCUITS

This biscuit is so called because its shape resembles that of an Afghan turban.

200 g butter
120 ml castor sugar
360 ml cake flour
pinch of salt
25 ml cocoa powder
100 ml cornflakes
100 ml chopped walnuts
100 g milk chocolate, melted

Preheat oven to 180 °C. Cream butter and sugar until light and fluffy. Add sifted flour, salt and cocoa and mix well. Stir in cornflakes and walnuts. Mixture should be of a soft dropping consistency. Drop spoonfuls (forming clusters) onto greased baking sheets and bake for about 15 minutes. Remove from baking sheet and allow to cool before drizzling with melted chocolate.
MAKES ABOUT 40.

SHORTBREAD SURPRISES

These are ideal for children's parties because of the surprise chocolate centre.

500 g butter
300 ml castor sugar
250 ml cornflour
5 ml baking powder
5 x 250 ml cake flour
6 large Tex chocolates

Preheat oven to 180 °C. Cream butter and sugar until light and fluffy. Sift together dry ingredients and add to creamed mixture to form a soft dough. Refrigerate for approximately 30 minutes. Divide dough in two and reserve half for another use. Roll out dough about 10 cm wide and as long as possible to form a long oblong roll. Place chocolate bars lengthwise down the centre of the oblong and fold dough around chocolate. Wrap oblong roll in waxed paper and refrigerate overnight before cutting into 1 cm slices. Bake for about 10–15 minutes or until brown.
MAKES ABOUT 60.

VARIATIONS
- Shape the reserved dough into biscuit-sized balls. Place a chocolate-covered almond nut or Brazil nutties in centre and fold dough in crescent shape around it. Bake as for Shortbread surprises.
- Add about 100 ml chopped walnuts to reserved dough mixture. Roll into oblong shape and refrigerate overnight. Cut into 1 cm slices and bake as for Shortbread surprises.

Centre: Pastry horns and Fancy puff pastries. Back row from left: Shortbread surprises (see variation, page 57), Coconut nests, a barakat with Coconut and Almond scraps, and Afghan biscuits.

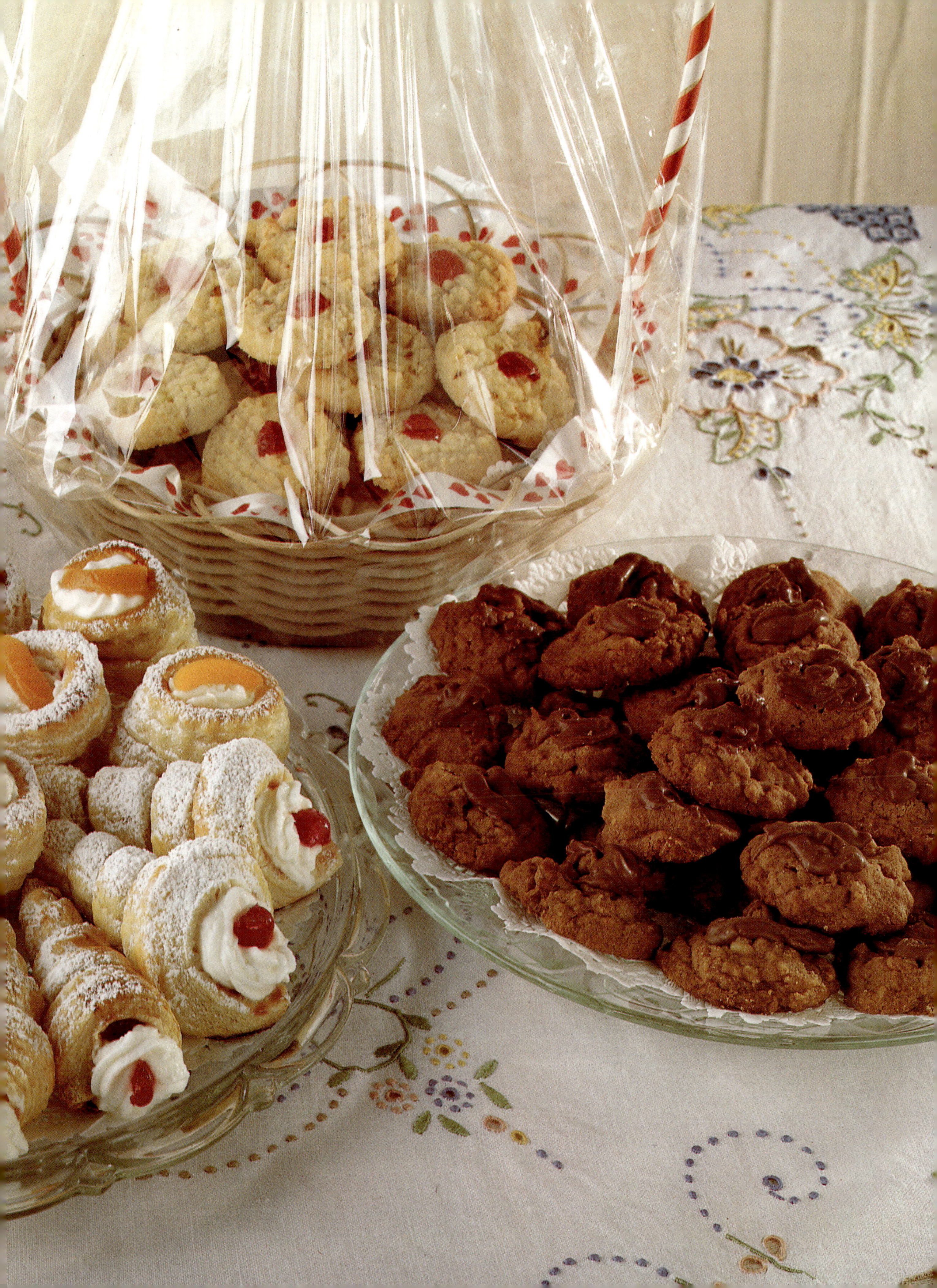

HONEY AND COCONUT BISCUITS

These delicious biscuits keep well if stored in an airtight container and can therefore be baked well in advance for a festive occasion.

125 g butter
125 ml sugar
1 egg, lightly beaten
30 ml desiccated coconut
30 ml honey
375 ml self-raising flour
250 ml desiccated coconut for coating

Preheat oven to 180 °C. Cream butter and sugar until light and fluffy. Fold in egg and mix well. Add 30 ml coconut and honey and beat until combined. Fold in sifted flour and mix well. Roll teaspoonfuls of mixture into balls and coat with coconut. Place on lightly greased baking sheets, at least 5 cm apart. Bake for about 15 minutes. Cool on wire racks.
MAKES ABOUT 36.

COCONUT NESTS

If you want to include these in a barakat, coat with finely chopped almonds instead of coconut.

115 g softened butter
65 ml sugar
1 egg, separated
320 ml cake flour
1 ml salt
desiccated coconut for coating
raspberry jam for filling

Preheat oven to 180 °C. Cream butter and sugar. Fold in beaten egg yolk and combine well. Sift flour and salt together and add to creamed mixture. Roll dough into tiny balls. Dip balls into lightly beaten egg white and coat with coconut. Place on lightly greased baking sheet and indent the centre of each biscuit with your thumb. Bake for 15–20 minutes. Allow to cool completely on wire racks before filling centre of each biscuit with raspberry jam.
MAKES ABOUT 40.

SHORTBREAD FINGERS

250 g butter
250 ml icing sugar
125 ml cooking oil
50 ml cornflour
750 ml cake flour
5 ml strawberry essence
200 g chocolate, broken into pieces

Preheat oven to 200 °C. Mix butter, icing sugar and oil together until light and fluffy. Add sifted cornflour and cake flour and strawberry essence and mix to a very soft dough, adding more flour if too sticky. Put mixture into a piping bag or cookie gun fitted with a small star tube. Pipe fingers onto a lightly greased baking sheet. Bake for about 10 minutes or until golden brown. Leave on sheets for about 5 minutes before turning out onto wire racks. Melt chocolate, then dip in ends of biscuits and leave on waxed paper to set.
MAKES ABOUT 120 FINGER BISCUITS.

VARIATION
Custard biscuits: Add 50 ml custard powder to dry ingredients. Pipe rosettes and decorate with a quarter glacé cherry, Smarties or hazelnuts before baking. Alternatively, pipe rosettes and bake plain. Decorate with melted chocolate and sprinkle with nuts.

GRANADILLA BISCUITS

185 g butter
5 ml finely grated lemon rind
200 ml icing sugar
pulp of 3 granadillas
200 ml cornflour
320 ml self-raising flour

ICING
125 ml sifted icing sugar
10 ml butter
pulp of 1 granadilla

Preheat oven to 190 °C. Cream together butter, lemon rind and sifted icing sugar until light and fluffy. Add granadilla pulp and mix well. Mix in sifted cornflour and self-raising flour. Put mixture in a piping bag fitted with a fluted tube. Pipe decorative shapes onto lightly greased baking sheets. Bake for 12–15 minutes or until golden brown. Turn out onto wire racks to cool completely. Meanwhile, combine ingredients for icing, stir over hot water and beat until smooth and glossy. Dip tops of biscuits in granadilla icing.
MAKES ABOUT 50 BISCUITS.

VARIATION
Instead of granadilla icing, use melted chocolate.

CHERRY NUT BALLS

Very attractive sweets to send to neighbours during Ramadan or to include in an engagement barakat.

125 g butter
65 ml sugar
1 egg
5 ml vanilla essence
250 ml self-raising flour
200 ml chopped mixed nuts
glacé cherries for decoration

Preheat oven to 180 °C. Cream butter and sugar until light and creamy. Fold in egg and vanilla essence and beat well. Add sifted flour and mix to a soft dough. Drop teaspoonfuls of mixture into nuts and roll into balls. Press half a cherry on top of each ball and place on lightly greased baking sheets, allowing about 2,5 cm between each ball for spreading. Bake for about 15 minutes or until golden brown. Cool slightly before removing from baking sheets. Cool on wire rack.
MAKES ABOUT 36.

MELT-IN-THE-MOUTHS

These are similar to the commercial variety but can be dipped in melted chocolate and sprinkled with nuts.

4 x 250 ml cake flour, sifted
250 ml icing sugar, sifted
15 ml cornflour
250 g butter
200 ml cooking oil

Preheat oven to 200 °C. Mix flour, icing sugar and cornflour together. Rub in butter and oil until dough sticks together. Shape dough into long oblong shape 4 cm thick by 4 cm wide and wrap in waxed paper. Refrigerate for about 1 hour. Remove covering and slice dough into fingers. Bake for 10–15 minutes. Cool on wire racks.
MAKES ABOUT 75.

FANCY PUFF PASTRIES

An important addition to any barakat.

750 g puff pastry (page 12)
1 egg, beaten

Preheat oven to 230 °C. Roll out pastry to a thickness of 3 mm on a lightly floured surface and cut into about 100 rounds (6 cm in diameter) with a biscuit cutter. Cut a 2,5 cm diameter hole in half the rounds. Moisten the whole rounds with cold water and place a round with a hole in it on top of each. Place on ungreased baking sheets and brush with egg. Bake for about 5 minutes. Reduce heat to 200 °C and bake a further 15 minutes or until light gold. Remove from baking sheets and cool on wire racks.
MAKES 50.

FILLINGS

- Spoon 5 ml strawberry jam into each hole and pipe swirls of fresh cream on top. Decorate with glacé cherries or fresh strawberries.
- Spoon 10 ml prepared instant pudding into each hole and top with whipped fresh cream.
- Spoon 5 ml caramel into each hole, add a slice of banana and top with whipped fresh cream. Sprinkle with grated Peppermint Crisp chocolate.
- Spoon about 10 ml Apple cream pie (page 70) filling into each hole and decorate with whipped fresh cream.

PASTRY HORNS

Use a savoury filling and turn these pastry horns into delicious snacks, ideal for a special occasion such as a formal dinner party.

500 g puff pastry (page 12)

FILLING
125 ml fresh cream, whipped
180 ml strawberry jam
glacé cherries and icing sugar for decoration

Preheat oven to 220 °C. Roll out pastry in an oblong shape about 2 mm thick. Cut into 1,5-cm-wide strips with a pastry wheel or sharp knife. Dampen strips with water. Roll damp side uppermost onto lightly greased horn shapes, starting at the pointed end. Overlap each new turn of pastry by about 5 mm. Place on an ungreased baking sheet with the end of pastry facing down. Sprinkle with castor sugar. Bake for 10–15 minutes. Gently remove horn shapes. Cool pastry horns on wire rack. Place about 5 ml jam inside each horn and pipe with cream. Decorate with a piece of glacé cherry and dust with icing sugar.
MAKES ABOUT 36.

Vanilla cream Swiss roll.

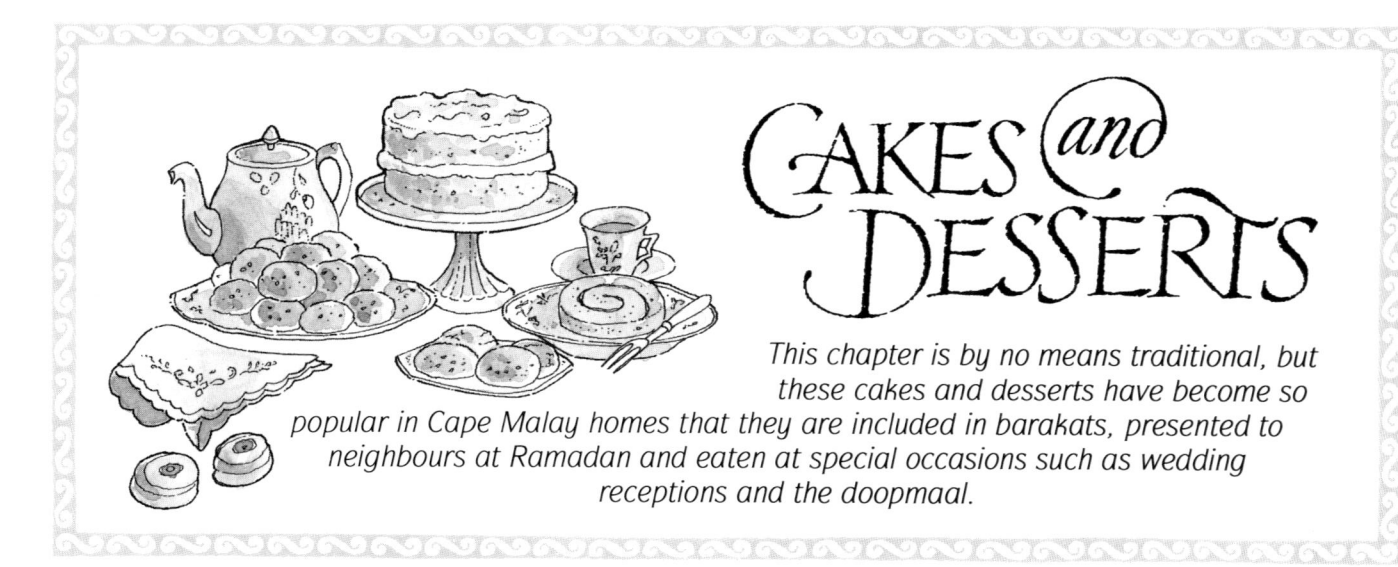

CAKES and DESSERTS

This chapter is by no means traditional, but these cakes and desserts have become so popular in Cape Malay homes that they are included in barakats, presented to neighbours at Ramadan and eaten at special occasions such as wedding receptions and the doopmaal.

VANILLA CREAM SWISS ROLL

No engagement barakat can be complete without a slice of this Swiss roll.

4 eggs, separated
125 ml castor sugar
30 ml hot water
60 g chocolate, grated
125 ml self-raising flour, sifted
30 ml castor sugar for sprinkling

VANILLA CREAM FILLING
200 ml fresh cream
10 ml icing sugar
5 ml vanilla essence

Preheat oven to 180 °C. Grease a 25 cm x 30 cm Swiss roll pan and line base with greaseproof paper. Beat egg yolks and 125 ml castor sugar for about 5 minutes or until thick and creamy. Blend hot water and chocolate, then add to egg mixture. Mix in flour and blend. Beat egg whites in separate bowl until soft peaks form and fold into chocolate mixture. Pour into pan and bake for about 12 minutes. Turn out immediately onto waxed paper which has been sprinkled with 30 ml castor sugar. Trim off crisp edges from sides of cake and roll up in greaseproof paper like a Swiss roll. Stand for about 2 minutes, unroll and set aside to cool. Beat together ingredients for filling. Spread cake with filling and roll up. Serve topped with whipped cream and chocolate flakes.
MAKES 1 SWISS ROLL.

VARIATION
- Spread 100 ml caramel condensed milk onto cake, top with sliced bananas and Vanilla cream filling. Roll up and decorate with caramel and whipped cream.
- Spread Swiss roll with strawberry jam and mix 250 ml sliced, fresh strawberries into filling.

TANGY ORANGE CAKE

150 g margarine or butter
250 ml castor sugar
2,5 ml grated orange rind
2 eggs, separated
500 ml cake flour
10 ml baking powder
pinch of salt
5 ml vanilla essence
175 ml freshly squeezed orange juice
75 ml water

ICING
60 ml freshly squeezed orange juice
125 ml water
grated rind of 1 orange
75 ml sugar
25 ml cornflour
1 egg, well beaten
25 ml margarine or butter

Preheat oven to 180 °C. Grease and line two 20 cm round cake pans. Cream margarine or butter and sugar, add orange rind and egg yolks, and beat well. Sift flour, baking powder and salt together and add to creamed mixture alternately with the vanilla essence, orange juice and water. Blend well. Whisk egg whites until soft peaks form, then add to creamed mixture. Divide equally between pans and bake for 25–30 minutes. Remove from oven and cool for about 5 minutes in pans before turning out onto wire rack to cool. For icing, combine orange juice, water, orange rind, sugar and cornflour in a saucepan and stir over moderate heat until it boils. Add a little of this mixture to the egg and mix well. Then pour it back into saucepan and bring to the boil while stirring constantly. Remove from heat, add margarine or butter and stir. Cool before filling cakes. Sandwich cakes together with half the filling and spread remainder on top.
MAKES 1 X 20 CM ROUND CAKE.

FRUIT-LAYERED CAKE

This cake is best served as soon as possible after baking.

125 g margarine or butter
200 ml castor sugar
2 extra-large eggs
5 ml vanilla essence
375 ml cake flour
10 ml baking powder
pinch of salt
125 ml milk

FILLING
500 ml fresh cream
50 ml castor sugar
2,5 ml vanilla essence
1 x 410 g can fruit cocktail, well drained
125 ml glacé cherries

Preheat oven to 180 °C. Grease and line two 20 cm round cake pans. Cream margarine or butter and sugar. Add eggs one at a time, blending well after each addition. Add vanilla essence and mix well. Add sifted dry ingredients alternately with milk and mix gently. Divide mixture equally between pans and bake for 25–30 minutes. Leave in pans for 5 minutes, then turn out onto wire racks to cool completely. Slice each layer in half horizontally. For the filling, whip cream with sugar and vanilla essence and divide in two. Combine half the fruit cocktail and half the filling and sandwich the layers of cake together. Cover the whole cake, including the sides, with the rest of the cream. Decorate top with cream rosettes, remaining fruit cocktail and glacé cherries.
MAKES 1 X 20 CM ROUND CAKE.

LIGHT FRUIT CAKE

An economical alternative to a rich glacé fruit cake.

300 ml sultanas
60 ml currants
60 ml seedless raisins
60 ml roughly chopped glacé cherries
100 ml flaked almonds
10 ml grated orange rind
250 g butter
160 ml castor sugar
160 ml packed brown sugar
750 ml cake flour
10 ml baking powder
2,5 ml ground cinnamon
5 ml ground mixed spice
1 ml grated nutmeg
5 eggs
20 ml lemon juice

Preheat oven to 150 °C. Grease and line a deep, round cake or loaf pan. Combine dried fruit, cherries, nuts and orange rind and sprinkle with 30 ml flour. Cream butter and sugar until light and fluffy. In a separate bowl, sift together rest of flour, baking powder and spices. Beat eggs into creamed mixture one at a time, following each addition with 15 ml of the flour mixture. Fold in remaining flour mixture, fruit and lemon juice and mix to blend well. Turn mixture into pan and bake for about 2 hours or until a skewer inserted in centre comes out clean. Leave for about 10 minutes before turning out onto wire rack to cool completely. Remove waxed paper and store in airtight cake tin.
MAKES 1 CAKE.

GRANADILLA CAKE

A delicious cake in which the sweet icing sugar balances the sour taste of the granadillas. Use fresh granadilla pulp if possible as this improves the flavour of the cake.

125 g butter
300 ml castor sugar
4 extra-large eggs, lightly beaten
500 ml cake flour
125 ml cornflour
15 ml baking powder
60 ml milk
60 ml water
60 ml granadilla pulp

FILLING
60 g soft butter
250 ml icing sugar
50 ml granadilla pulp

Preheat oven to 160 °C. Grease and line two 20 cm round cake pans. Cream butter and sugar and gradually add beaten eggs. Sift dry ingredients together and add to creamed mixture alternately with milk and water mixture, mixing gently to blend well. Stir in granadilla pulp. Mixture should be of soft, dropping consistency. Divide mixture equally between pans. Bake for 35–40 minutes. Leave in pans for about 5 minutes before turning out onto wire racks to cool completely. Combine filling ingredients and mix well. Sandwich cakes together with filling and sprinkle top with icing sugar.
MAKES 1 X 20 CM ROUND CAKE.

UPSIDE-DOWN PINEAPPLE CAKE

For a more festive dessert, place cherries and cashew nuts between pineapple rings.

175 ml brown sugar
200 g margarine or butter
1 x 450 g can pineapple rings
125 ml white sugar
2 extra-large eggs
500 ml cake flour
10 ml baking powder
pinch of salt

Preheat oven to 180 °C. Grease a deep, 22 cm round cake pan. Cream brown sugar and 75 g margarine or butter. Line bottom and sides of pan with sugar mixture. Drain pineapple rings, reserving juice. Place pineapple rings on sugar mixture. Cream 125 g margarine or butter and white sugar until light and fluffy. Add eggs one at a time, beating well after each addition. Sift flour, baking powder and salt together and add to creamed mixture alternately with pineapple juice and blend gently. Pour mixture over pineapple rings and bake for 1 hour. Remove from oven and turn onto serving dish immediately. Serve hot with whipped cream.
MAKES 1 X 22 CM ROUND CAKE.

GOLDEN COCONUT CAKE

This cake keeps well for up to three days.

125 g margarine or butter
125 ml sugar
3 egg yolks
5 ml vanilla essence
250 ml cake flour
10 ml baking powder
125 ml milk

TOPPING
3 egg whites
125 ml sugar
250 ml desiccated coconut

Preheat oven to 160 °C. Grease and line a deep, 20 cm round cake pan. Cream margarine or butter and sugar. Gradually add egg yolks and vanilla essence and beat well. Sift together flour and baking powder and add to creamed mixture alternately with milk. Mix well. Spread mixture into pan. For the topping, whisk egg whites until stiff peaks form, slowly add the sugar and beat until stiff. Mix in coconut, spoon onto cake mixture and bake for 50–60 minutes. Stand for about 10 minutes before turning out onto wire rack to cool.
MAKES 1 X 20 CM ROUND CAKE.

CARAMEL AND CREAM SPONGE CAKE

125 g margarine
250 ml castor sugar
3 eggs, lightly beaten
450 ml cake flour
15 ml baking powder
30 ml cornflour
5 ml vanilla essence
125 ml water

TOPPING
250 ml fresh cream, whipped
250 ml caramel condensed milk

Preheat oven to 175 °C. Grease and line two 20 cm round cake pans. Cream margarine and sugar well and gradually add eggs. Sift dry ingredients together and add to creamed mixture alternately with vanilla essence and water. Blend well. Divide mixture equally between pans and bake for 30–35 minutes. Leave in pans for about 5 minutes before turning out onto wire racks to cool completely. Sandwich cakes together with a layer of caramel condensed milk and cream. For topping, pipe rows of caramel alternating with rows of cream rosettes.
MAKES 1 X 20 CM ROUND CAKE.

PINEAPPLE COCONUT CAKE

125 g butter
10 ml grated lemon rind
250 ml castor sugar
2 extra-large eggs
125 ml desiccated coconut
500 ml self-raising flour
200 ml pineapple juice

FROSTING
50 g butter, very soft
400 ml icing sugar
50 ml pineapple juice
glacé or canned pineapple for garnishing

Preheat oven to 180 °C. Grease and line a 20 cm round cake pan. Cream butter, lemon rind and sugar until light and fluffy. Add eggs one at a time, beating well until combined. Stir in coconut, half the sifted flour, half the pineapple juice, then remaining flour and pineapple juice. Stir until well blended. Pour mixture into pan and bake for about 1 hour. Turn out onto wire rack to cool completely. For the frosting, mix together the butter, icing sugar and pineapple juice until smooth. Spread the frosting over cake and decorate with glacé pineapples or drained pineapple pieces.
MAKES 1 X 20 CM ROUND CAKE.

MOIST COCONUT CAKE

This cake keeps well for up to three days, and is particularly popular with children who fancy the coconut frosting.

125 g butter
2,5 ml coconut or almond essence
250 ml castor sugar
2 eggs
125 ml desiccated coconut
375 ml self-raising flour, sifted
250 ml sour cream
85 ml milk

FROSTING
500 ml icing sugar, sifted
375 ml desiccated coconut
2 egg whites, lightly beaten
pink food colouring

Preheat oven to 180 °C. Grease and line a deep, 23 cm round cake pan. Cream butter, coconut or almond essence and sugar until light and fluffy. Add eggs one at a time and beat well until combined. Stir in half the coconut and sifted flour with half the sour cream and milk, then stir in remaining ingredients, blending until smooth. Pour mixture into pan and bake for about 1 hour. Stand in pan for about 10 minutes before turning out onto wire rack to cool completely. For the frosting, mix together the icing sugar, coconut and egg whites, then tint with pink food colouring. Spread frosting on top of cooled cake.
MAKES 1 X 23 CM ROUND CAKE.

SPONGE FLANS

An economical and oil-free sponge that can be filled with a variety of fillings to suit almost any occasion.

3 extra-large eggs
250 ml castor sugar
300 ml self-raising flour, sifted
45 ml water

Preheat oven to 180 °C. Beat eggs and castor sugar until mixture leaves a trail when lifted. Add sifted self-raising flour and water and beat until smooth. Grease a flan pan very well and sprinkle lightly with flour. Pour mixture into pan and bake for about 15 minutes.
MAKES 1 FLAN.

FILLINGS
- Fill with caramel condensed milk and banana and kiwi fruit slices. Top with fresh cream and grated chocolate.
- Fill with a layer of thick custard, top with drained fruit cocktail and kiwi fruit, and decorate with fresh cream.

LEMON BUTTER CAKE

This cake keeps well for up to three days.

½ x 250 g carton cream cheese
250 g butter
10 ml grated lemon rind
375 ml castor sugar
3 eggs
375 ml cake flour, sifted

LEMON GLACÉ
250 ml icing sugar, sifted
10 ml lemon juice

Preheat oven to 180 °C. Grease a 20 cm ring pan very well and sprinkle with flour. Beat cream cheese, butter and lemon rind together until smooth. Add sugar and beat until light and fluffy. Add eggs one at a time and beat. Stir in flour, beating lightly until smooth. Pour mixture into ring pan and bake for 30 minutes. Reduce temperature to 160 °C and bake a further 30 minutes. Leave in pan for about 10 minutes before turning out onto wire rack to cool completely. Mix together lemon glacé ingredients to a smooth pouring consistency and pour over cake.
MAKES 1 X 20 CM RING CAKE.

CARAMEL SPONGE CAKE

A quick and easy Ramadan treat for a busy mother as it only takes about 15 minutes to bake.

4 eggs
250 ml castor sugar
300 ml self-raising flour, sifted
5 ml baking powder, sifted
20 ml cooking oil
5 ml vanilla essence
30 ml water

TOPPING
125 ml caramel
1 banana, sliced and sprinkled with lemon juice
250 ml whipped cream
grated chocolate for garnishing

Preheat oven to 200 °C. Beat eggs and castor sugar until thick and creamy. Add flour, baking powder, oil and vanilla essence and beat until smooth. Add water and blend well. Pour mixture into well-greased and lined Swiss roll pan and bake for 12–15 minutes. Turn onto wire rack to cool and remove paper from bottom. Spread with caramel. Top with slices of banana and decorate with cream and chocolate. Cut into 5 cm squares.
SERVES 10–15.

Clockwise from front: Upside-down pineapple cake, Light fruit cake and Sponge flans with a variety of fillings.

CAKES AND DESSERTS • 67

MARSHMALLOW CHEESECAKE

CRUST
250 ml Marie or Tennis biscuit crumbs
40 ml melted margarine
40 ml condensed milk

FILLING
400 g pink and white marshmallows
90 ml fresh milk
2 x 250 g carton cream cheese
15 ml lemon juice
250 ml fresh cream, whipped
2–3 drops pink food colouring
60 g chocolate, broken into pieces

Grease and line a 22 cm round, loose-bottomed cake pan. Mix crumbs, margarine and condensed milk together and line the cake pan. Refrigerate until required. Meanwhile, cut marshmallows into small pieces, reserving about 12 whole ones for decoration. Put marshmallows into a saucepan with milk and melt over low heat, stirring constantly. Leave to cool. Beat cheese and lemon juice in a bowl. Stir in marshmallow mixture and blend until smooth. Fold in cream, add food colouring and mix. Spoon onto biscuit base and leave to set in refrigerator for 2–3 hours. To decorate, halve marshmallows and arrange around edge of cheesecake. Melt chocolate over hot water and drizzle over centre of cheesecake.
MAKES 1 X 22 CM ROUND CAKE.

Microwave tip
Place chocolate in corner of oven bag, microwave on 80% for about 2 minutes or until chocolate has melted, pressing bag occasionally to ensure chocolate is melting evenly. Snip a small corner from the bag and use as a piping bag.

CHOCOLATE ORANGE CAKE

This cake keeps well and is ideal to use as a basis for a child's birthday cake.

125 g butter, very soft
15 ml grated orange rind
3 eggs
440 ml self-raising flour
340 ml castor sugar
125 ml cocoa powder
2,5 ml bicarbonate of soda
125 ml fresh orange juice
65 ml water

TOPPING
125 ml caramel
250 ml fresh cream, whipped

Preheat oven to 180 °C. Grease a deep, 20 cm x 20 cm square cake pan. Combine all ingredients for cake in a large bowl, beat on low speed with electric mixer for 3 minutes or until mixture has changed colour and is smooth. Pour mixture into pan and bake for about 1 hour. Stand for 5–10 minutes before turning out onto wire rack to cool completely. Top cake with caramel and cream.
MAKES 1 X 20 CM SQUARE CAKE.

CHOCOLATE MARBLE CAKE

This very showy cake with its unusual marshmallow and chocolate topping is perfect for a birthday cake.

125 g butter
5 ml vanilla essence
125 ml castor sugar
30 ml golden syrup
625 ml self-raising flour, sifted
375 ml milk
30 ml cocoa powder

TOPPING
100 g pink and white marshmallows
100 g chocolate, broken into pieces
15 ml butter

Preheat oven to 180 °C. Lightly grease a deep, 20 cm round spring-form pan. Cream butter, vanilla essence, sugar and syrup until light and fluffy. Stir in half the flour with half the milk, then stir in remaining flour with 60 ml milk and blend well. Place half the mixture into a separate bowl, stir in cocoa and rest of milk. Drop alternate spoonfuls of each mixture into prepared pan. Run a knife through the mixture to give a marbled effect. Bake for about 45 minutes. Remove cake from oven, top with a layer of marshmallows and bake a further 5 minutes, or until marshmallows start to melt. Cool for about 10 minutes before removing from pan. Meanwhile, melt chocolate and butter together and mix well. Drizzle chocolate mixture over marshmallows.
MAKES 1 X 20 CM ROUND CAKE.

APPLE CAKE

125 g butter
250 ml castor sugar
3 eggs
375 ml self-raising flour, sifted
1 x 410 g can pie apples

CARAMEL SAUCE
125 ml sugar
60 g butter
200 ml milk
10 ml caramel essence

Preheat oven to 180 °C. Grease a 23 cm x 28 cm rectangular cake pan. Cream butter and sugar until light and fluffy. Add eggs one at a time, beating well after each addition. Add self-raising flour and mix well. Pour batter into pan and arrange pie apples on top. Bake for about 20 minutes or until golden brown. Meanwhile, mix caramel sauce ingredients in a saucepan and boil, uncovered, for about 5 minutes or until syrup is thick. Pour hot syrup over cake and grill for 3–5 minutes. Cut into 18 squares and serve decorated with whipped cream rosettes.
SERVES 18.

CHERRY AND SULTANA LOAF

*The sour cream provides a moist and long-lasting quality to this loaf, a slice of which is an important addition to a **ghajad barakat**, a gift presented when special prayers are held.*

375 ml self-raising flour
200 ml cake flour
125 g butter
10 ml grated lemon rind
250 ml castor sugar
3 eggs
125 ml sliced glacé cherries
125 ml chopped sultanas
200 ml sour cream
65 ml fresh lemon juice

Preheat oven to 180 °C. Grease and line a 14 cm x 20 cm loaf pan. Sift together both flours and set aside until required. Cream butter, lemon rind and sugar until light and fluffy. Beat in eggs one at a time until well blended. Stir in fruit and half the flour. Combine sour cream and lemon juice. Add half the sour cream mixture to creamed mixture, then stir in remaining flour and sour cream. Pour into pan and bake for 1–1¼ hours. Stand for about 10 minutes in pan before turning out onto wire rack to cool completely. Wrap loaf in clingwrap or foil to prevent it from drying out.
MAKES 1 LOAF.

BOILED CARROT LOAF

This deliciously flavoured and moist carrot loaf can also be served as a dessert with hot custard.

250 ml finely grated carrots
200 ml chopped raisins or sultanas
200 ml water
200 ml castor sugar
30 g butter
2,5 ml ground cinnamon
2,5 ml grated nutmeg
2,5 ml bicarbonate of soda
200 ml self-raising flour
200 ml cake flour
125 ml chopped walnuts or pecan nuts

Preheat oven to 160 °C. Grease and line a 14 cm x 20 cm loaf pan. Combine carrots, raisins or sultanas, water, sugar, butter, cinnamon and nutmeg in deep saucepan and stir constantly over medium heat until sugar is dissolved. Bring to the boil, reduce heat, cover and simmer for about 10 minutes over low heat. Set aside to cool completely. Stir in soda and half the sifted flours, then add remaining flours and walnuts or pecan nuts. Pour mixture into pan. Bake for about 1 hour. Stand for about 5 minutes before turning out onto wire rack to cool. Serve sliced with butter.
MAKES 1 LOAF.

BANANA AND WALNUT LOAF

This loaf keeps well and is nice to take on a long journey or camping trip.

200 ml self-raising flour
200 ml cake flour
2,5 ml bicarbonate of soda
125 g butter
5 ml ground cinnamon
200 ml castor sugar
2 extra-large eggs
250 ml mashed ripe bananas
125 ml chopped walnuts or pecan nuts

Preheat oven to 180 °C. Grease and line two small loaf pans. Sift together both flours and soda and set aside until required. Cream butter, cinnamon and sugar until light and fluffy. Add eggs one at a time and beat until well blended. Stir in half the banana with half the sifted dry ingredients, then stir in remaining banana and dry ingredients. Add walnuts or pecan nuts and mix well. Spread equal quantities of mixture evenly into pans and bake for about 40 minutes. Stand for about 5 minutes before turning out onto wire rack to cool. Serve sliced with butter.
MAKES 2 SMALL LOAVES.

APPLE MERINGUE DELIGHT

This hot tart is ideal for cold winter days.

1 x 410 g can pie apples
10 ml brown sugar
2,5 ml ground cinnamon
60 ml raisins
1 x 225 g can evaporated milk
30 ml custard powder
30 ml castor sugar

MERINGUE
2 egg whites
100 ml castor sugar

Preheat oven to 200 °C. Chop pie apples into pieces, add brown sugar, cinnamon and raisins and mix well. Place pie filling in greased ovenproof dish. Combine evaporated milk and enough water to make up 375 ml. Mix custard powder and castor sugar to a smooth paste with a little of the diluted milk. Heat remaining milk in deep saucepan over medium heat. When milk is almost boiling, pour over paste and stir well. Pour custard into a clean saucepan and cook, uncovered, over low heat for 3–5 minutes or until thick. Pour hot custard over apple filling in the pie dish. To make meringue, whisk egg whites until stiff, whisk in half the castor sugar, then fold in remaining castor sugar. Pipe or pile meringue onto apple filling and bake for 3–5 minutes or until golden brown in colour.
MAKES 1 PIE.

APPLE CREAM PIE

PASTRY
315 ml cake flour
2,5 ml salt
2,5 ml ground cinnamon
65 ml sugar
5 ml baking powder
10 ml grated lemon rind
125 ml butter or margarine
1 egg

FILLING
2 large Granny Smith apples
2 eggs
125 ml sugar
30 ml cake flour, sifted
10 ml grated lemon rind
125 ml fresh cream
1 x 250 g carton cream cheese
15 ml mixed peel (optional)
65 ml raisins or sultanas, chopped
1 ml salt

Preheat oven to 180 °C. Grease a fairly deep 30 cm x 18 cm cake pan. For the pastry, sift together dry ingredients, add lemon rind and cut in butter or margarine, using two knives. Add egg and mix well to form a smooth ball. Roll out pastry on floured surface. Line base of pan with pastry. For the filling, peel and core apples, cut into quarters, then into thin slices. Arrange in overlapping lines in pastry shell. Beat eggs and sugar until thick. Gradually add rest of ingredients for filling and mix well. Pour mixture over apples and bake for about 1 hour. Serve hot or cold, topped with whipped cream and sprinkled with cinnamon.
MAKES 1 PIE.

VANILLA SQUARES WITH GRANADILLA

Quick and easy to make and ideal to give to neighbours at Ramadan.

1 x 250 g packet coconut or Tennis biscuits
300 ml thick cream
250 ml fresh milk
1 x 90 g packet instant vanilla pudding

ICING
250 ml icing sugar
pulp of 2 granadillas
5 ml soft butter

Cover base of 23 cm x 23 cm cake pan with biscuits, with the patterned sides facing down. Combine cream and milk in large bowl, add vanilla pudding and beat with rotary or electric mixer for about 1 minute or until smooth. Pour pudding mixture over layer of biscuits. Top with a single layer of biscuits, patterned sides facing up. Combine icing ingredients in small bowl and stir over hot water until icing is spreadable. Spread icing over filling and refrigerate overnight before cutting into squares.
MAKES ABOUT 20.

Cook's tip
When positioning the second layer of biscuits, make sure they correspond with the bottom layer, thus making it easier to cut into squares.

Clockwise from left: Vanilla squares with granadilla, Apple cream pie and Apple cake.

CAKES AND DESSERTS • 71

TROPICAL FRUIT TRIFLE

The kiwi fruit and mangoes impart a delicious flavour to this tropical trifle.

1 Swiss roll, sliced
2 x 80 g packets pineapple jelly powder
400 ml boiling water
400 ml cold water
1 litre prepared custard
250 ml fresh cream
5 ml vanilla essence
15 ml icing sugar
pulp of 3 granadillas
3 kiwi fruits, sliced
1 fibreless mango, sliced

Line base of glass serving dish with Swiss roll slices. Dissolve jelly in boiling water, add cold water and stir well. Refrigerate until thick and syrupy. Pour jelly over Swiss roll and refrigerate until jelly is set. Pour custard over and refrigerate for a further 30 minutes. Whip cream, vanilla essence and icing sugar until soft peaks form. Spread a layer of cream over custard. Decorate with rest of cream, granadilla pulp, kiwi fruit and mango slices.
SERVES 6–8.

VARIATION
Before refrigerating the jelly, add 1 x 410 g can well-drained fruit cocktail.

BANANA, CUSTARD AND CREAM DELIGHT

A convenient and easy alternative to trifle when catering for a children's party.

2 x 125 g packets Boudoir biscuits
150 ml caramel condensed milk
500 ml hot, thick custard
6 large ripe bananas
1 x 90 g packet instant vanilla pudding
1 x 410 g can evaporated milk, chilled
250 ml fresh cream, whipped
chocolate curls or vermicelli for decoration

Spread biscuits with caramel condensed milk and pack them on the base of a large rectangular dish. Spoon hot custard over biscuits and allow to cool. Slice bananas and arrange on top of custard. Beat instant pudding and evaporated milk together for about 1 minute or until smooth and thick. Pour pudding over custard layer. Decorate with fresh cream rosettes and chocolate curls or vermicelli. Refrigerate for about 1 hour before serving.
SERVES 10–12.

TROPICAL FRUIT TART

BASE
½ x 200 g packet Marie biscuits, crushed
25 ml desiccated coconut
75 ml melted butter or margarine

FILLING
1 x 410 g can fruit cocktail
2 eggs, beaten
1 x 225 g can condensed milk
25 ml lemon juice

Preheat oven to 180 °C. Mix ingredients for base and press into a 20 cm round pie dish. Chop fruit where necessary, add rest of ingredients and mix to blend well. Pour over biscuit base and bake for 15 minutes. Serve garnished with fresh cream rosettes.
SERVES 6–8.

LEMON MERINGUE COCONUT SLICES

BASE
90 g butter
30 ml castor sugar
200 ml cake flour, sifted
85 ml cornflour, sifted

FILLING
1 x 397 g can condensed milk
2 eggs, separated
10 ml grated lemon rind
125 ml freshly squeezed lemon juice
65 ml sugar
125 ml desiccated coconut
100 ml flaked almonds or desiccated coconut

Preheat oven to 180 °C. Grease and line a 20 cm x 28 cm lamington pan. Cream butter and sugar until light and fluffy. Gradually add flour and cornflour. Turn out onto lightly floured surface and knead until smooth, about 5 minutes. Spread evenly over base of pan. Bake for about 15 minutes. For the filling, combine condensed milk, egg yolks, lemon rind and juice in a bowl. Pour over base and bake for about 10 minutes. Beat egg whites until soft peaks form. Gradually add sugar and beat until dissolved. Stir in coconut. Spread meringue over lemon filling and sprinkle with flaked almonds or coconut. Bake a further 10 minutes or until golden brown. Cool in pan before cutting into squares.
MAKES ABOUT 20 SQUARES.

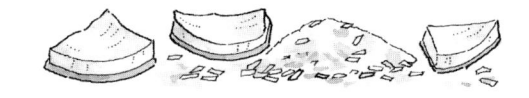

72 • *MORE CAPE MALAY COOKING*

These small cakes are popular centrepieces for cake platters.

TRI-COLOUR SNOWBALLS

*Another favourite served at **ghajad** (special prayers).*

125 g butter or margarine
50 ml cooking oil
250 ml castor sugar
5 ml vanilla essence
3 extra-large eggs
500 ml self-raising flour
2,5 ml baking powder
60 ml milk
a few drops pink food colouring
a few drops green food colouring

COATING
250 ml smooth apricot jam
100 ml hot water
500 ml desiccated coconut

Preheat oven to 190 °C. Cream butter or margarine, oil and sugar until light and fluffy. Add vanilla essence and stir. Add eggs one at a time, beating well after each addition. Sift together flour and baking powder. Add half the flour and half the milk to creamed mixture, then add rest of flour and milk. Divide mixture into three: colour one pink, one green and leave one neutral. Use only a few drops at a time to ensure that colour is not too dark. Grease patty pans very well and drop a spoonful of each colour into each pan. Bake for 10–15 minutes or until golden brown. Leave cakes to cool slightly before turning out onto wire racks to cool completely. For the coating, mix jam and water in a small saucepan and simmer until jam has melted, about 5 minutes, stirring often. Place coconut in paper or plastic bag. Using a slotted spoon, dip each cake into jam sauce coating, drain and sprinkle with coconut.
MAKES ABOUT 30.

CHOCOLATE CREAM PUFFS

250 ml hot water
125 g margarine
250 ml cake flour, sifted
4 large eggs
10 ml cocoa powder, sifted

FILLING
1 x 397 g can caramel condensed milk
250 ml fresh cream, whipped

TOPPING
100 ml castor sugar
100 ml cocoa powder

Preheat oven to 200 °C. Place water and margarine in saucepan and bring to the boil. Quickly add flour and stir with a wooden spoon until mixture leaves sides of saucepan. Remove from heat and let mixture cool slightly. Add eggs one at a time, beating well after each addition. Beat in cocoa and blend well. Put teaspoonfuls of mixture on lightly greased baking sheets, allowing room for spreading. Bake for about 10 minutes. Reduce heat to 180 °C and bake a further 30 minutes or until puffs are crisp. Remove from oven, make small slits in sides of puffs to let steam escape. Return puffs to oven for about 5 minutes to dry out. Allow puffs to cool completely before filling. For filling, put caramel into piping bag fitted with long nozzle. Pipe a little caramel and cream into each puff. Dust puffs with topping made up of castor sugar and cocoa sifted together.
MAKES 50.

VARIATION
Spitz cookies: Omit cocoa powder and fry spoonfuls in deep hot oil. Roll in Cinnamon sugar (page 52) while still warm.

BUTTERFLY CAKES

These fancy cakes are used as centrepieces for cake platters at Malay weddings.

125 g butter or margarine
200 ml castor sugar
5 ml vanilla essence
2 extra-large eggs
375 ml self-raising flour, sifted
125 ml milk

FILLING
90 ml strawberry jam
125 ml fresh cream
icing sugar to dust
glacé cherries or strawberry slices for decoration

Preheat oven to 180 °C. Cream butter or margarine, sugar and vanilla essence until light and creamy. Add eggs one at a time, beating well after each addition. Stir in half the flour and half the milk, then stir in rest of flour and milk. Spoon mixture into greased patty pans, about two-thirds full. Bake for about 10 minutes or until golden brown. Turn out onto wire rack and allow to cool. Cut out a circle from the top of each cake to a depth of about 2 cm, reserving circles. Place a little jam in each cavity and pipe with whipped cream. Replace 'wings' (circles cut in half) at angles. Dust with sifted icing sugar and decorate with glacé cherries or strawberry slices. Put each cake into a paper case.
MAKES ABOUT 18.

CAKES AND DESSERTS • 73

CUSTARD TARTLETS

*A popular treat served to well-wishers when pilgrims leave for Mecca. These tartlets can also be served at a **doopmaal** (meal served at babies' naming ceremonies) instead of the traditionally served melktert.*

1 kg apple tartlet dough

FILLING
10 eggs
130 ml sugar
1 litre milk
3 pieces stick cinnamon
3 cardamom pods, slightly bruised
30 ml custard powder
15 ml cornflour
10 ml vanilla essence
5 drops almond essence
5 ml ground cinnamon or grated nutmeg

Preheat oven to 160 °C. Roll out dough and line well-greased patty pans, using up all the dough. For filling, beat eggs and 125 ml sugar until well blended. Mix 50 ml milk with custard powder, cornflour and 5 ml sugar to form a paste. Heat remaining milk with cinnamon sticks and cardamom pods and simmer for about 10 minutes, then remove the cinnamon and cardamom. Stir hot milk into custard paste and return to stove, stirring constantly to form a thin runny custard. Pour custard into egg mixture, add vanilla and almond essence and mix well. Spoon mixture into dough-lined patty pans. Dot with butter and sprinkle with cinnamon or nutmeg. Bake for about 15 minutes, or until custard is set. Leave in pans for at least 5 minutes before turning out onto wire rack.
MAKES 48.

FRUIT TARTLETS

470 ml cake flour
1 ml salt
100 g butter
1 egg
15 ml castor sugar

FILLING
25 ml butter
50 ml cake flour
15 ml castor sugar
1 egg yolk
150 ml milk
2,5 ml vanilla essence
1 x 410 g can fruit of choice, drained
75 ml smooth apricot jam
250 ml fresh cream, whipped
glacé cherries for garnishing

Sift flour and salt together in a bowl. Rub in butter, then stir in egg and castor sugar. Form into dough, adding a little cold water if necessary. Chill for about 20 minutes. Roll out thinly between two sheets of plastic. Cut out rounds to fit tartlet pans. Prick all over with fork and bake blind at 180 °C for about 15 minutes. Cool on a wire rack. For the filling, melt butter in a saucepan and stir in flour and sugar. Beat egg yolk and milk and pour into the pan. Cook over moderate heat, stirring, until the mixture comes to the boil. Remove from heat and stir for 1 minute, then add vanilla essence. Cool and spoon into pastry cases. Top with fruit and brush with sifted, heated apricot jam. Garnish with cream rosettes and cherries.
MAKES ABOUT 12 TARTLETS.

APPLE TARTLETS

These tartlets freeze well.

BASE
(Makes 1 kg dough)
250 g butter or margarine
60 ml cooking oil
200 ml castor sugar
2 egg yolks
5 ml vanilla essence
250 ml self-raising flour
750 ml cake flour
pinch of salt

FILLING
1 x 410 g can pie apples, chopped
15 ml brown sugar
5 ml ground cinnamon
60 ml seedless raisins or sultanas
250 ml icing sugar to dust

Preheat oven to 190 °C. Cream butter or margarine, oil and sugar until light and fluffy. Add egg yolks one at a time, beating well after each addition. Stir in vanilla essence. Sift flours and salt together and mix into creamed mixture to make a soft dough. Roll out about 5 mm thick on a lightly floured surface. Cut out rounds with an 8 cm round fluted biscuit cutter, reserving a third of the dough for grating on top. Place rounds in greased patty pans. Meanwhile, in a large saucepan, combine filling ingredients and cook, uncovered, for about 10 minutes over moderate heat, stirring to blend well. Allow filling to cool completely. Drop about 10 ml apple filling into each patty pan. Grate reserved dough on top. Bake for 12–15 minutes or until golden brown. Allow to stand in pans for about 5 minutes before turning out onto wire racks. Dust with sifted icing sugar and serve with whipped cream.
MAKES 48.

Clockwise from front: Fruit tartlets, Butterfly cakes, Boeber and Tri-colour snowballs.

CAKES AND DESSERTS • 75

BEVERAGES

Ending a meal on a sweet note is an indulgence we all enjoy. The beverages in this section, however, do not only apply to the end of a meal but can be enjoyed any time of the day as they are – subject to Muslim dietary laws – free of alcohol. Fruit is the main ingredient in most of the beverages and is usually combined with milk, ice-cream or juice, but can easily be adapted to suit your taste. Also included is a healthy tropical punch for 36 people – a favourite drink at informal gatherings. When serving beverages, choose generous-sized glasses, brush their rims with egg white and then dip them into coloured jelly crystals.

MANGO JUICE

This drink is sold in cafés in Mecca and has become a popular drink among Cape Malays.

3 ripe stringless mangoes
125 ml castor sugar (or to taste)
125 ml ice water

Peel and slice mangoes. Liquidize all ingredients together in blender or food processor. Add more ice water if desired. Serve in tall glasses with ice-cubes.
SERVES 4.

SPANSPEK SHAKE

Spanspek shake is normally of thick consistency and is therefore ideal for a dessert. If served as a drink, it may be necessary to add more cold milk.

1 ripe medium spanspek or winter melon
5 scoops vanilla ice-cream
500 ml fresh milk, chilled

Peel and slice spanspek. Liquidize all ingredients in blender or food processor. Serve immediately.
SERVES 4.

ZOE'S FIZZY GINGER BEER PUNCH

A refreshing drink ideal for informal gatherings, but when served at a children's party, substitute 1 litre club soda for 1 litre ginger beer.

2,5 litres ginger beer, chilled
1 x 110 g can granadilla pulp
1 x 410 g can crushed pineapple
750 ml granadilla squash
mint leaves for garnishing

Mix together the ginger beer, granadilla pulp, pineapple and granadilla squash in a large punch bowl and garnish with mint leaves. Serve chilled on crushed ice.
SERVES 12.

FRESH FRUIT JUICE

This juice does not keep well, so it is advisable to make it on a daily basis.

7 large oranges
2 lemons
1 pineapple
500 ml ice water
2,5 ml salt (or to taste)
60 ml sugar (or to taste)

Squeeze out juice from oranges and lemons and discard the pips. Peel pineapple and cut into chunks. Liquidize pineapple with water. Combine all the ingredients in a large bowl and add more water if necessary. Serve chilled.
SERVES 6.

76 • MORE CAPE MALAY COOKING

TROPICAL FRUIT PUNCH

Ideal for Eid or when lots of guests pop in.

1 pineapple or 1 x 410 g can crushed pineapple
¼ watermelon
2 bananas
juice of 5 oranges
juice of 2 lemons
pinch of salt
1 x 110 g can granadilla pulp
750 ml orange or granadilla squash
1 litre guava juice
1 litre granadilla juice
2 litres soda water
mint leaves for garnishing

Skin pineapple, watermelon and bananas, cut into chunks and liquidize. Add rest of ingredients, except mint leaves, and mix. Serve chilled, in tall glasses and garnished with mint leaves.
SERVES 36.

SPICED ORANGE JUICE

An aromatic and spicy drink, especially delicious when served hot on cold winter days.

500 ml freshly squeezed orange juice
5 whole cloves
5 ml grated orange rind
30 ml honey
1 piece stick cinnamon
orange slices for decoration

Combine all ingredients in a saucepan and bring to the boil. Simmer, covered, for about 5 minutes. Sieve mixture through thin gauze or fine sieve. Serve hot or chilled, in glasses decorated with orange slices.
SERVES 2.

ROSE SYRUP

Traditionally served during Ramadan, this syrup is delicious mixed with milk.

5 x 250 ml sugar
1,25 litre water
7,5 ml lemon juice
pinch of citric acid
15 ml red food colouring
30 ml rose-water

Dissolve sugar in water in a deep heavy-based saucepan. Bring to the boil, then add lemon juice. Allow to boil again but do not stir. Skin off the scum carefully. Add citric acid and cook until the mixture turns to syrup (not too thick). Set aside to cool, then add colouring and rose-water and bottle. To serve, combine 10 ml syrup and 250 ml cold milk.
MAKES 2,5 LITRES SYRUP.

VARIATION
For each serving, add a scoop vanilla ice cream and liquidize until frothy. Serve immediately.

ALMOND MILK

A nutritious drink for the frail and elderly.

50 ml ground almonds
1 litre fresh milk
3 cardamom pods, bruised
15 ml honey (or to taste)

Boil almonds in milk with cardamoms over medium heat until well blended, about 20 minutes. Stir in honey. Strain into glasses and serve hot or chilled.
SERVES 6.

PEPPERMINT COFFEE

Instead of dessert, serve this delicious hot coffee with biscuits (see Biscuits and Pastries, page 55).

500 ml fresh milk
500 ml water
30 ml condensed milk
20 ml pure instant coffee
2,5 ml peppermint oil
fresh cream, whipped (optional)

Combine milk, water and condensed milk and bring to the boil. Add coffee and stir well, then add peppermint oil and mix until well blended. Serve in glass mugs and garnish with whipped cream.
SERVES 6.

Clockwise from back right: Pot-roast leg of lamb with Stuffed gem squash and Crispy potatoes, Mutton breyani and Crayfish curry on a bed of white rice.

78 • MORE CAPE MALAY COOKING

Eid Celebration Dinner

The Festival of Charity or **Eidul-fitr** is celebrated on the night following the conclusion of Ramadan, and the Feast of Sacrifice or **Eidul-Adha** is usually celebrated about 70 days after Ramadan. These are the most festive of occasions, when charity is given to the poor by those Muslim households who can afford it. Special attention and care is taken in preparing foods for Eid. Dishes such as Crayfish curry, Mutton breyani, Pot-roast leg of lamb, trifle and punch are reserved for this day. Depending on the season in which Eid falls, the warmer foods may be replaced by cold chicken and sambals.

Menu

Pot-roast leg of lamb
Mutton breyani
Crayfish curry on a bed of white rice (page 21)
Glazed baby carrots
Stuffed gem squash
Almond yellow rice
Crispy potatoes
Beetroot and onion salad

♦

Fruit trifle

♦

Tropical fruit punch (page 77)

POT-ROAST LEG OF LAMB

For Eid, this roast is garnished with peaches and pitted prunes piped with fresh cream.

**1 x 2 kg leg of lamb
cooking oil for browning
200 ml water
5 pickling onions
10 baby potatoes
30 ml cake flour**

**MARINADE
10 ml salt
10 ml freshly ground black pepper
5 ml crushed, dried red chillies
15 ml crushed garlic
30 ml fresh lemon juice
30 ml cooking oil
5 bay leaves**

Wash meat well and make deep gashes in it with a sharp knife. Combine all the marinade ingredients and brush marinade over leg and into gashes. Heat a little oil in a wide, deep saucepan and brown leg on all sides. Add water and roast, covered, over medium heat for 30–45 minutes. Add pickling onions and cook until meat is done, about 30 minutes. Remove leg and onions from saucepan and add baby potatoes. Cook until potatoes are tender, about 10 minutes, stirring frequently. Remove potatoes and keep warm with meat and onions. Mix flour with gravy in saucepan and bring to the boil while stirring, adding more water if required. Slice meat and serve with onions and gravy.
SERVES 10.

MUTTON BREYANI

A dish of Indian origin adopted by the Malay community, which is also served at weddings.

1 kg mutton or lamb, cubed
15 ml grated fresh root ginger
10 ml crushed garlic
5 ml salt
250 ml brown lentils
625 ml long-grain brown rice or basmati rice
250 ml cooking oil
300 ml hot water
6 potatoes, peeled and quartered
3 large onions, thinly sliced
6 hard-boiled eggs, halved, for garnishing

MARINADE
3 pieces stick cinnamon
5 cardamom pods
2 whole green chillies
2,5 ml borrie (turmeric)
5 ml roasted masala
30 ml garam masala
5 whole cloves
5 whole allspice
a few strands saffron
1 large tomato, skinned and grated
250 ml buttermilk

Wash and drain meat in a colander. Rub ginger, garlic and salt into meat. Combine marinade ingredients and marinate meat for about 3 hours. Boil lentils until tender, about 20 minutes. Rinse and drain. Wash rice until water runs clear and drain. Heat 50 ml oil in a large saucepan over medium heat, add rice and toss to coat well. Add 100 ml hot water and cook, covered, over medium heat for 5 minutes. Remove from stove and set aside. Heat remaining oil in a large, deep saucepan and fry potatoes until browned, about 4 minutes. Remove potatoes from saucepan and set aside. Add onions and fry until brown and crisp, 7–8 minutes. Reserve a quarter of the onions for garnishing. Add meat and spices to remaining onions and cook, covered, for about 30 minutes. Remove meat from saucepan and set aside. In the same saucepan, layer ingredients in the following order: potatoes, half the rice, meat, lentils, and finally the remaining rice. Top with reserved onions. Dot with butter and sprinkle with 200 ml hot water. Cook, covered, over high heat for 5 minutes, then simmer for 45 minutes to 1 hour over low heat. Garnish with hard-boiled eggs and serve with atjars and Tomato and onion salad (page 84).
SERVES 10–12.

VARIATIONS
- Use cubed chicken fillets instead of mutton and cook for approximately 30 minutes, or until chicken is cooked through.
- Fry 1 seeded and sliced green pepper with onions before adding meat and spices.

GLAZED BABY CARROTS

50 ml butter or margarine
45 ml brown sugar
2,5 ml salt
pinch of chilli powder
50 ml water
500 g baby carrots, peeled
100 ml slivered blanched almonds (optional)
2,5 ml ground cinnamon

Melt butter or margarine in a saucepan over medium heat and stir in sugar, salt, chilli powder and water. Add carrots and stir to coat completely. Reduce heat and simmer, covered, until carrots are tender, about 12–15 minutes. Add almonds and cook a further 2 minutes. Serve sprinkled with ground cinnamon.
SERVES 6.

STUFFED GEM SQUASH

10 small gem squash
50 ml butter
5 ml grated nutmeg
dry spicy corn (page 43) for filling

Remove tops of gem squash, serrating edges if possible. Remove seeds, and wash well. Boil in lightly salted water for about 10 minutes. Drop 5 ml butter into each squash, sprinkle with nutmeg and fill with Dry spicy corn (page 42).
SERVES 10.

ALMOND YELLOW RICE

For a fruity variation, use raisins or sultanas instead of the almonds.

500 ml water
250 ml long-grain rice
2 pieces stick cinnamon
4 cardamom pods
2,5 ml borrie (turmeric)
5 ml salt
100 ml blanched almonds
50 ml sugar
50 ml butter or margarine

Bring water to the boil. Add rice, cinnamon, cardamom, borrie and salt and cook, uncovered, until quite soft, about 15 minutes. Rinse and drain in a colander. Return rice to saucepan with almonds and sugar and dot with butter. Steam, covered, over medium heat for about 10 minutes, turning lightly with a fork every now and then.
SERVES 6–8.

VARIATION
Add 100 ml raisins or sultanas with almonds, or substitute almonds with 100 ml desiccated coconut.

Microwave tip
For fluffier rice, microwave on 50% for about 5 minutes instead of steaming.

CRISPY POTATOES

10 medium potatoes, peeled
50 ml cooking oil or melted butter
5 ml chilli powder
10 ml paprika
250 ml grated cheese (optional)

Preheat oven to 200 °C. Boil potatoes in lightly salted water for about 5–10 minutes. Drain off excess water and cool. Cut potatoes into 1 cm-thick slices, keeping base intact. Brush with melted butter or oil and sprinkle with paprika and chilli powder. Place on greased baking sheet and bake until potatoes are crispy, about 30 minutes. Sprinkle with cheese and grill for about 3 minutes or until golden brown and cheese has melted.
SERVES 6–8.

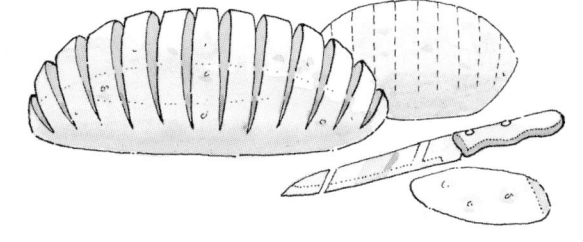

BEETROOT AND ONION SALAD

1 bunch beetroot
2 medium onions, thinly sliced
20 ml salt
15 ml sugar
250 ml brown vinegar
5 ml crushed, dried red chillies

Cover beetroot with water and boil until tender, about 45 minutes. Peel and grate beetroot finely. Sprinkle onions with salt, pour boiling water over and drain. Rinse with cold water and drain, squeezing out excess moisture. Dissolve sugar in vinegar. Combine all ingredients in a salad bowl and stir to combine.
SERVES 10–12.

VARIATION
Add a peeled and grated green apple.

Cook's tip
Slice beetroot instead of grating.

FRUIT TRIFLE

Old-fashioned trifle is an all-time favourite in the Malay community. It is served at Eid and is sometimes included in a bride's dinner basket.

1 Swiss roll
1 x 80 g packet raspberry jelly
1 x 80 g packet greengage jelly
500 ml boiling water
300 ml cold water
1 x 410 g can fruit cocktail, drained
500 ml prepared custard
125 ml flaked almonds
250 ml fresh cream
10 glacé cherries for garnishing
a few pieces of angelica for garnishing

In two separate containers, dissolve each jelly in 250 ml boiling water. Add 150 ml cold water to each and stir. Set aside to cool. Line bottom and sides of glass bowl with Swiss roll slices. Spoon 30 ml jelly over each slice, alternating the colours. Allow to set in freezer for about 20 minutes. Spoon well-drained fruit on top of Swiss roll slices, then pour remaining greengage jelly over. Set in freezer, then pour raspberry jelly on top and allow to set. Finally, pour custard over and sprinkle with almonds, reserving a few for decoration. Whip cream until stiff, then spread a layer over the custard. Pipe remaining cream on top and decorate with reserved almonds, cherries and angelica. Leave in the refrigerator for 2–3 hours to set.
SERVES 6–8.

BRIDE'S DINNER BASKET

Of all the Malay feasts, weddings are still the most elaborate. Traditionally, the bride is presented with a 'dinner basket' – a sign of affection when the bridegroom's family sends her dinner. This basket comprises traditional foods, wrapped in cellophane and decorated with pretty bows and flowers. Many couples choose to forego this expensive custom, but this chapter shows just how easy it really is to prepare traditional Cape Malay dishes. For more colour and variety, I have included a rainbow jelly and a very special bread basket.

Menu

MEATS:
Bobotie
Denningvleis
Sosatie chops
Mutton curry
Pot-roast leg of lamb (page 79)
Mutton breyani (page 80)

SIDE DISHES:
Mashed potatoes
Indian Puris
Stuffed gem squash (page 80)
Glazed baby carrots (page 80)
Almond yellow rice (page 81)

SALADS:
Tomato and onion salad
Mixed fruit and vegetable salad
Beetroot and onion salad (page 81)

BREADS:
Bread basket

DESSERTS:
Gestoofde droë vrugte
Strawberry pudding
Potato pudding
Rainbow jelly
Fruit trifle (page 81)

BOBOTIE

*The word 'bobotie' is derived from the Indonesian word **bobotok** and is a light-textured curried meat loaf topped with a golden savoury custard.*

2 slices stale white bread, crusts removed
30 ml cooking oil
1 onion, thinly sliced
2,5 ml ground cloves
5 ml crushed garlic
5 ml salt
10 ml curry powder
5 ml borrie (turmeric)
500 g steak mince
2 eggs
30 ml hot water
20 ml lemon juice
30 ml sugar

TOPPING
1 egg, lightly beaten
150 ml milk
4 bay or lemon leaves for garnishing

Preheat oven to 160 °C. Soak bread in water for 10 minutes, then squeeze dry. Heat oil in a large frying pan and braise onion until golden, 5–10 minutes. Add cloves, garlic, salt, curry powder and borrie and simmer for 5 minutes. Add to mince with eggs, hot water, lemon juice and sugar and mix to combine well. Spoon mixture into well-greased ovenproof dish and bake for 40 minutes, or until golden brown. Remove from oven. Beat egg and milk well and pour over bobotie. Add bay or lemon leaves and bake at 180 °C for 5–10 minutes, or until custard is set.
SERVES 6.

DENNINGVLEIS

There is no other name in any language for this popular traditional Malay dish. At first glance it looks like ordinary lamb stew, but it has a delicious sweet-and-sour flavour and an enticing aroma.

1 x 1 kg leg of lamb
500 g onions, thinly sliced

MARINADE
5 cloves garlic, crushed
5 ml crushed, dried red chillies
5 ml salt
2,5 ml freshly ground black pepper
3 bay leaves
5 whole allspice
15 ml sugar (or to taste)
20 ml brown vinegar

Wash meat very well, then cut meat into small chunks. Combine the marinade ingredients and rub into meat. Set aside for 1 hour. Combine onions and meat in a large saucepan and braise, covered, over medium heat until meat is well-done, about 45 minutes. If the denningvleis gets too dry, add a little water (no more than 250 ml) and stir. Serve hot with gem squash, Mashed potatoes and Almond yellow rice (page 81).
SERVES 4–6.

SOSATIE CHOPS

This oil-free sosatie recipe is based on the traditional one, but is much quicker and easier to prepare.

1 kg lamb chops
500 g onions, thinly sliced

MARINADE
10 ml crushed garlic
3 bay leaves
3 whole cloves
1 green chilli, finely chopped
5 ml borrie (turmeric)
30 ml curry powder
45 ml sugar
5 ml salt
60 ml lemon juice or vinegar

Combine the marinade ingredients and marinate chops for 1 hour. Place meat and marinade in a saucepan with onions and cook, covered, over medium heat for 45 minutes to 1 hour, or until meat is tender. Serve with Mashed potatoes and boiled vegetables.
SERVES 6.

MUTTON CURRY

This mutton curry has a thick, tasty gravy and should be served with rotis or puris.

500 g mutton or lamb, cubed
5 ml crushed garlic
10 ml grated fresh root ginger
5 ml ground jeera (cumin)
5 ml ground koljander (coriander)
3 pieces stick cinnamon
3 cardamom pods
4 whole cloves
5 ml borrie (turmeric)
5 ml chilli powder
5 ml salt
30 ml cooking oil
2 large onions, thinly sliced
150 ml water
250 ml grated or finely chopped tomato
2,5 ml sugar (optional)
3 medium potatoes, halved
250 ml hot water
60 ml chopped dhunia (coriander) leaves

Wash and drain meat. Combine with spices and salt. Heat oil in a large saucepan and braise onions for 5–10 minutes, or until golden brown. Add meat and 150 ml water and cook over medium heat until meat and spices are well blended, about 30 minutes. Add tomato and sugar and cook a further 10 minutes, or until tomato is absorbed into gravy. Add potatoes and hot water and cook until potatoes are soft, about 15 minutes, adding more hot water if thinner gravy is desired. Sprinkle with dhunia leaves and cook for a further 2 minutes before serving.
SERVES 4–6.

VARIATION
Add 250 ml canned peas before adding dhunia leaves.

MASHED POTATOES

600 g potatoes, peeled and quartered
2,5 ml salt
45 ml butter
125 ml hot milk
5 ml baking powder
2,5 ml grated nutmeg for garnishing
10 ml chopped parsley for garnishing

Cook potatoes, covered, in salted water until tender, 15–20 minutes, then drain. Add butter and hot milk and mash to a smooth consistency. Add baking powder and beat until fluffy. Serve garnished with nutmeg and parsley.
SERVES 4.

INDIAN PURIS

Although puris are generally served with curries, they are also very tasty spread lightly with butter and jam.

500 ml cake flour
2,5 ml salt
175 ml melted butter or ghee (clarified butter)
100 ml warm milk
100 ml water
500 ml cooking oil

Sift flour and salt. Rub butter into flour to make a crumbly mixture. Combine milk and water, add to flour mixture and mix to a soft dough. Moisten hands with a little oil and knead dough until smooth and elastic. Break off small pieces of dough the size of ping-pong balls and roll out on a lightly floured surface into circles about 7 cm in diameter. Heat oil until fairly hot and deep-fry puris, two or three at a time, until puffed and golden brown on both sides, about 1 minute. Press puris into oil with a slotted spoon to ensure that they puff up. Remove from oil and drain on paper towel. Serve hot or cold.
MAKES ABOUT 18–20.

Cook's tip
Drained and cooled puris keep well in an airtight container for up to one week.

TOMATO AND ONION SALAD

1 large onion, very thinly sliced
5 ml salt
500 ml hot water
2 large ripe tomatoes, chopped
5 ml crushed, dried red chillies
10 ml sugar
30 ml white vinegar

Sprinkle onion with salt, and rub it in well. Pour hot water over and leave to drain in a colander. Squeeze out excess moisture. Combine onion with remaining ingredients.
SERVES 4–6.

MIXED FRUIT AND VEGETABLE SALAD

This fresh-tasting combination is best served immediately.

1 medium pineapple, peeled and coarsely chopped
1 red apple, cored and chopped
1 Granny Smith apple, cored and chopped
2 carrots, grated
60 ml seedless raisins
1 small English cucumber, thinly sliced
1 green pepper, seeded and cubed
a few lettuce leaves, shredded
1 avocado, peeled, stoned and sliced
a little lemon juice

Combine pineapple, apple, carrots, raisins, cucumber, green pepper and lettuce leaves in a salad bowl. Garnish with avocado slices sprinkled with lemon juice and serve.
SERVES 8.

BREAD BASKET

This edible and attractive basket makes an ideal container for smaller rolls but can also be used for cold meats or fruit.

500 ml warm water
60 ml sugar
20 ml active dried yeast
8 x 250 ml cake flour
10 ml salt
50 ml cooking oil
3 eggs, beaten
milk for brushing
poppy or sesame seeds for topping

Pour 120 ml warm water into a jug. Stir in 10 ml of the sugar and then sprinkle in the yeast. Cover and leave to froth. Sift flour and salt together and add remaining sugar. Make a well in centre of flour mixture and stir in yeast mixture, then add oil, eggs and remaining water. Mix to a workable dough, adding more water if necessary. Turn onto floured board and knead until smooth and elastic, about 10 minutes. Shape into a ball and place in a lightly oiled bowl, turning dough around so that it is oiled all over. Cover with plastic and leave to rise until doubled in size, about 1½ hours. Punch down, cover and leave to rise again until doubled. Divide dough into three equal portions. Roll out one portion into round shape about 25 cm in diameter. Place on greased baking sheet. Divide the second portion into three and roll into long sausages. Make a plait to fit around diameter of base. Pinch ends firmly together and fit plait onto base to form a frame. Divide the third portion into three and roll into long sausages, then plait to form a bow-shaped handle. Place on separate greased baking sheet.

Cover all the dough with plastic and leave to rise for about 30–45 minutes. Brush handle with milk and sprinkle with seeds. Bake at 190 °C on middle shelf of oven for 25 minutes or until golden brown. Brush outsides of base and frame with milk. Bake at 190 °C on middle shelf of oven for about 35 minutes, or until golden brown. Cool on wire rack. Assemble basket by securing handle, base and frame with toothpicks.
SERVES 6.

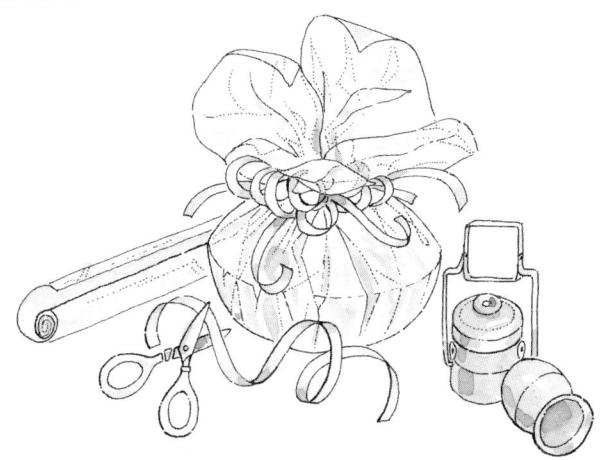

GESTOOFDE DROË VRUGTE

250 ml sugar
250 ml water
2 pieces stick cinnamon
1 x 250 g packet mixed dried fruit

Boil sugar, water and cinnamon until thick and syrupy, about 30 minutes. Add dried fruit and cook over medium heat for a further 15 minutes. Serve with hot puddings.
SERVES 6.

Cook's tip
To reduce cooking time, soak fruit in water for 1 hour.

STRAWBERRY PUDDING

1 x 80 g packet strawberry jelly
250 ml boiling water
1 x 410 g can evaporated milk, refrigerated overnight
250 ml fresh cream
500 ml strawberry yoghurt
30 ml castor sugar

Dissolve jelly in boiling water and allow to cool completely. Whip evaporated milk until thick and creamy, add jelly and blend well. Meanwhile, whip fresh cream separately, add to jelly mixture and blend well. Add yoghurt and castor sugar and mix until thoroughly combined. Pour into jelly mould and refrigerate until set. Serve with whipped cream and fresh strawberries.

POTATO PUDDING

*This unusual but very popular Malay pudding can be served at a **doopmaal** (meal served at babies' naming ceremonies) instead of the traditionally served melktert.*

1 kg potatoes
50 ml butter
1 litre milk
5 cardamom pods
3 pieces stick cinnamon
10 eggs, well-beaten
125 ml sugar
5 ml salt
10 ml vanilla essence
5 drops almond essence

Preheat oven to 180 °C. Cook potatoes until soft, then drain and mash with butter. Heat milk with cardamom pods and cinnamon and simmer until lukewarm, about 10 minutes, then remove the cardamom and cinnamon. Add the lukewarm milk to beaten eggs, combine with mashed potatoes and rest of ingredients. Pour into a well-greased ovenproof dish and bake for about 45 minutes, or until set and lightly golden. Serve with Gestoofde droë vrugte.
SERVES 8–10

VARIATION
Decorate with blanched almonds and cherries.

RAINBOW JELLY

Ideally this pudding should be prepared in a clear glass bowl to show off the rainbow colours.

1 x 80 g packet each of pineapple, strawberry and greengage jelly powder
1½ x 80 g packets lemon jelly powder
1 x 410 g can evaporated milk
1 x 410 g can fruit cocktail

Prepare pineapple, strawberry and greengage jellies separately according to instructions on packets. Set aside to cool completely. Dissolve lemon jelly in 200 ml boiling water and set aside to cool. Whip evaporated milk and mix with cooled-off lemon jelly, stirring to blend well. Drain fruit cocktail. Spoon half the fruit cocktail into jelly mould, cover with half the pineapple jelly and leave to set in freezer, about 30 minutes. Add a layer of milk and jelly mixture and leave to set again, about 30 minutes. Add half the strawberry jelly and leave to set, about 20 minutes. Add a layer of the milk mixture and leave to set. Continue in the same pattern until jelly and milk mixtures have been used up. When set, turn out onto platter and serve with whipped fresh cream.
SERVES 8.

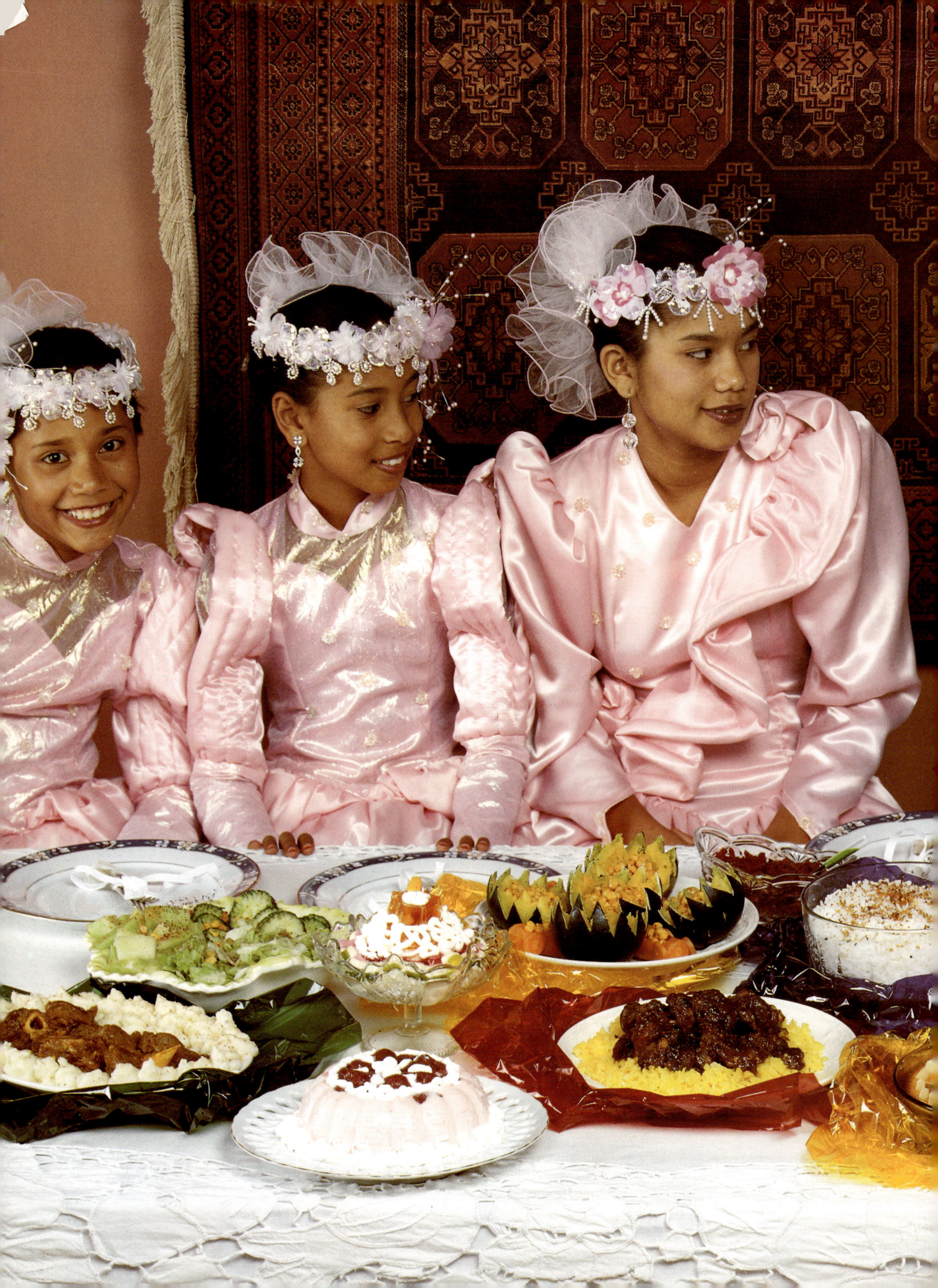

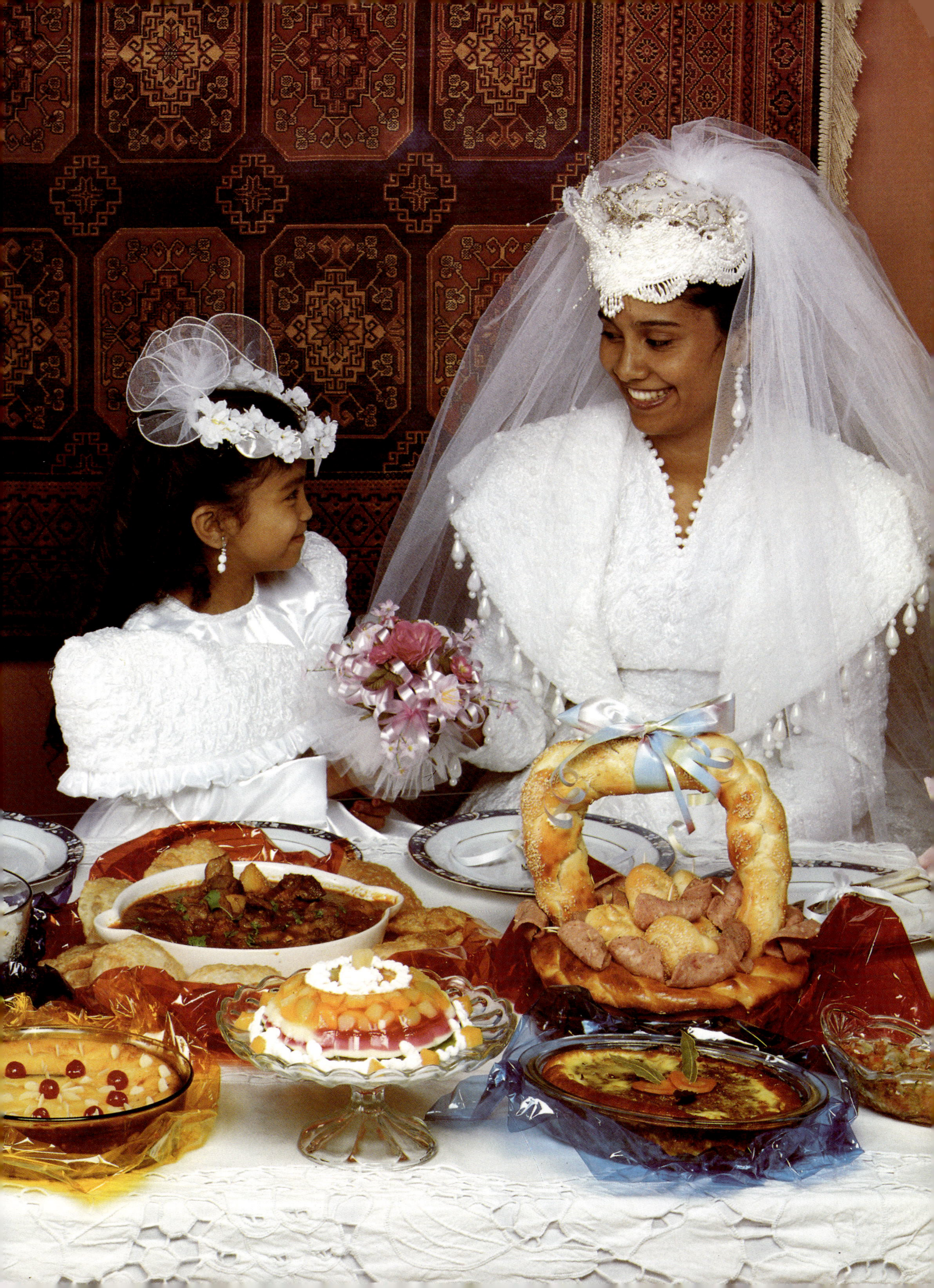

CATERING FOR LARGE NUMBERS

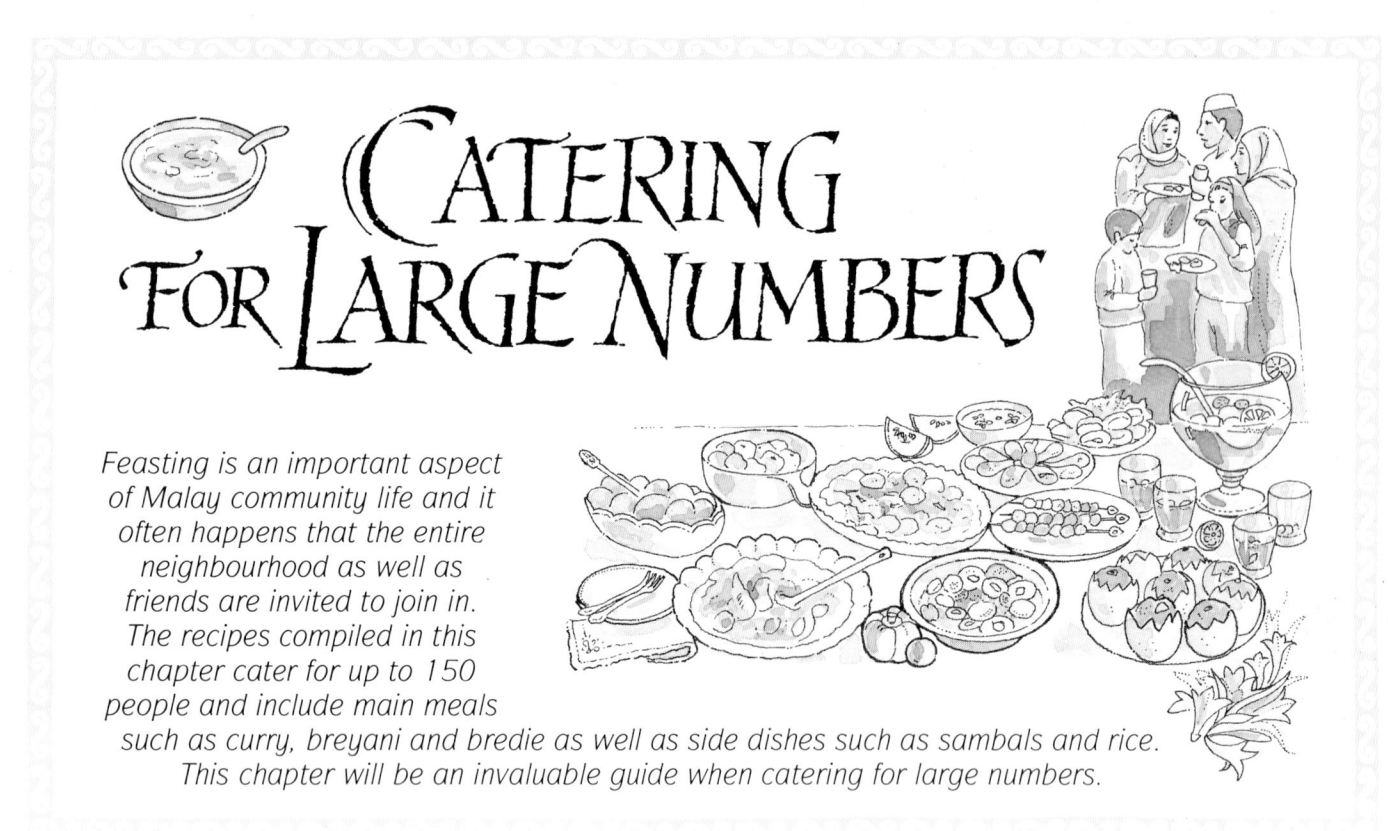

Feasting is an important aspect of Malay community life and it often happens that the entire neighbourhood as well as friends are invited to join in. The recipes compiled in this chapter cater for up to 150 people and include main meals such as curry, breyani and bredie as well as side dishes such as sambals and rice. This chapter will be an invaluable guide when catering for large numbers.

MAVROU

This hot spicy dish made with cubed steak is a favourite of the Cape Malays and is normally served at weddings.

15 kg beef steak, cubed
75 ml salt
75 ml ground jeera (cumin)
75 ml ground koljander (coriander)
60 ml ground barishap (fennel)
60 ml crushed, dried red chillies
75 ml grated fresh root ginger
60 ml crushed garlic
36 whole cloves
36 whole allspice
15 pieces stick cinnamon
1 x 10 g box saffron
500 ml cooking oil
8 kg onions, thinly sliced
12 large tomatoes, skinned and grated
sugar to taste (optional)

Combine all spices and toss with meat. Heat oil in large, deep saucepan, add onions and braise until golden, about 20–25 minutes. Add meat and spice mixture and cook, covered, over moderate heat until tender, about 1–1½ hours. Add tomatoes and cook a further 30 minutes, adding sugar if desired. Serve hot on a bed of Gesmoorde rys (page 91) with sambals and atjars.

SERVES 100–120.

SUGAR BEAN BREDIE

*This traditional Malay **lang sous** (gravy) bredie is always served at funerals.*

7 kg sugar beans, soaked overnight
2 litres water
400 ml cooking oil
6 kg onions, thinly sliced
12 kg mutton, cut into chunks
100 ml crushed garlic
6 whole green chillies
45 ml sugar (or to taste)
6 large tomatoes, skinned and grated
250 ml tomato paste
60 ml salt (or to taste)
50 ml crushed, dried red chillies
15 ml freshly ground black pepper

Boil sugar beans in water until soft, set aside but do not drain off excess water. Heat oil in large, deep saucepan and braise onions until golden brown, about 20 minutes. Add meat, garlic and green chillies and cook for about 45 minutes, stirring frequently. Mix in sugar, tomatoes, tomato paste, salt, dried chillies and black pepper and cook a further 15 minutes. Add cooked sugar beans and excess water and cook over moderate heat until meat is tender, about 30 minutes, stirring frequently to avoid sticking. Serve with white rice and Tomato and onion sambal (page 91).

SERVES 100–120.

MUTTON BREYANI

A dish of Indian origin which has been adopted by the Malay community and is usually served at weddings.

15 kg mutton, cut into chunks
150 ml grated fresh root ginger
100 ml crushed garlic
50 ml salt
2,5 kg brown lentils
7,5 kg long-grain brown rice or basmati rice
2 litres cooking oil
3 litres hot water
10 kg potatoes, peeled and quartered
200 g butter
10 kg onions, thinly sliced
8 dozen hard-boiled eggs for garnishing (optional)

MARINADE
15 pieces stick cinnamon
45 cardamom pods
15 whole green chillies
20 ml borrie (turmeric)
60 ml roasted masala
400 ml garam masala
35 whole cloves
35 whole allspice
saffron to taste
12 large tomatoes, skinned and grated
2,5 litres buttermilk

Wash and drain meat in colander. Combine ginger, garlic and salt and rub into meat. Mix together marinade ingredients and marinate meat for about 3 hours. Boil lentils until tender, about 30 minutes, then rinse and drain in colander. Wash rice until water runs clear, about 4–5 times, and drain. Heat 400 ml oil in large, deep saucepan, add rice and toss with slotted spoon until well coated with oil. Add 1 litre hot water and cook, covered, for 15 minutes, stirring frequently. Remove from stove. Heat remaining oil in large, deep saucepan and fry potatoes until browned. Remove potatoes from saucepan and set aside. Add 100 g butter to oil and fry onions until golden brown and crisp, 15–20 minutes. Reserve about a quarter of the onions for garnishing. Add marinated meat and spices to remaining onions and cook, covered, for 1 hour or until meat is fairly tender. Add potatoes to saucepan with meat, then lentils and lastly rice. Garnish with onions and dot with butter. Sprinkle remaining hot water over. Cook, covered, over high heat for 10 minutes, then simmer over low heat for 1 hour or until meat and rice are cooked. Serve with atjars and Tomato and onion sambal (page 91).
SERVES 150.

VARIATION
Use cubed chicken fillets instead of the mutton and cook for approximately 30 minutes.

Cook's tip
To save time, liquidize tomatoes, then add buttermilk.

MUTTON CURRY

This traditional curry is usually served with white rice and atjars at Malay funerals.

500 ml cooking oil
6 kg onions, thinly sliced
15 kg mutton, cut into chunks
120 ml crushed garlic
150 ml grated fresh root ginger
12 green chillies, finely chopped
36 pieces stick cinnamon
50 cardamom pods
50 whole cloves
60 ml ground jeera (cumin)
60 ml ground koljander (coriander)
200 ml roasted masala
50 ml borrie (turmeric)
60 ml salt (or to taste)
2 litres water
12 large tomatoes, skinned and grated
30 ml sugar (optional)
250 ml tomato paste
10 kg potatoes, peeled and cubed
3 bunches chopped dhunia (coriander) leaves

Heat oil in very large saucepan and braise onions until golden brown, about 20 minutes. Add meat, garlic, ginger, chillies, cinnamon, cardamoms and cloves and braise, covered, for about 30 minutes. Mix in spices and cook a further 30 minutes, stirring frequently. Add rest of ingredients, except potatoes and dhunia leaves, and cook a further 15 minutes over medium heat. Add potatoes and cook for 15 minutes or until potatoes are soft, then stir in dhunia leaves. Serve with white rice and atjars.
SERVES 100–120.

When pounding large quantities of ginger, add a little salt to prevent the ginger from becoming too slippery.

90 • *MORE CAPE MALAY COOKING*

WORTEL EN ERTJIE BREDIE

Although time-consuming to prepare, carrot and pea bredie is a popular and economic dish, traditionally served at Cape Malay funerals.

400 ml cooking oil
6,5 kg onions, chopped
15 kg mutton, cut into chunks
30 ml sugar (optional)
15 bunches carrots
6 kg potatoes
4 kg frozen peas
60 ml salt (or to taste)
100 ml crushed garlic
75 ml crushed, dried red chillies
±2 litres water
30 ml ground nutmeg
1 bunch freshly chopped parsley

Heat oil in large, deep saucepan and braise onions until golden brown, about 30 minutes. Wash and drain meat, then add to onions and braise until dark brown and nearly tender, about 1 hour. Add sugar (if using) to brown meat faster. Meanwhile, peel carrots and slice into julienne strips. Peel potatoes and cut in half. Add carrots, potatoes and peas to meat and cook, covered, over medium heat for about 35 minutes. Stir in salt, garlic and chillies and add enough water to make a gravy of desired thickness. Add nutmeg and parsley and cook for a further 15 minutes, or until well blended. Serve with white rice and atjars.
Serves 100-120.

VARIATION
Instead of frozen peas, use fresh peas if available.

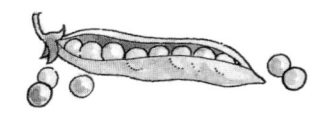

GESMOORDE RYS

A favourite accompaniment to curries, breyanis and bredies.

100 g butter
100 ml cooking oil
3,5 kg onions, thinly sliced
10 pieces stick cinnamon
30 cardamom pods
15 whole cloves
1 kg green peppers, seeded and sliced
7,5 kg uncooked long-grain rice
10 litres water
75 ml salt (or to taste)

Heat butter and oil in a very large, deep saucepan and braise onions until golden brown, about 25 minutes. Add spices and green peppers and cook a further 15 minutes. Wash rice until water runs clear, about 4–5 times, and drain. Add rice and water to onion and pepper mixture, sprinkling salt in between. Steam, covered, over moderate heat for about 1 hour, tossing occasionally with large wooden spoon, taking care not to break up rice grains. Alternatively, cover and steam in oven at 180 °C for about 1½ hours. Serve as a side dish.
SERVES 100–120.

CUCUMBER SAMBAL

6 large English cucumbers
50 ml salt
50 ml crushed green chilli
300 ml white vinegar
20 ml crushed garlic
50 ml sugar

Peel and grate cucumbers, sprinkle with salt and allow to draw for 15 minutes. Squeeze out excess moisture and combine cucumber with remaining ingredients. Serve with hot curries or breyanis.
SERVES 100.

TOMATO AND ONION SAMBAL

10 large onions, very thinly sliced
50 ml salt
20 large tomatoes, chopped
50 ml crushed, dried red chillies
5 green peppers, seeded and chopped (optional)
50 ml sugar
300 ml white vinegar

Sprinkle onions with salt and rub in well. Pour hot water over and leave to drain. Rinse in cold water and squeeze out excess moisture. Combine onions with remaining ingredients and mix well. Serve with hot curries or breyanis.
SERVES 100.

Outdoor Entertaining

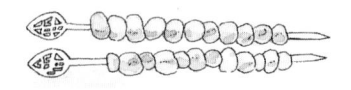

In South Africa the braai has become part of everyday life. The Cape Malays have taken to this form of outdoor entertaining in a big way. Although they occasionally eat boerewors, they are more partial to marinated chops, chicken and snoek – a favourite especially when entertaining visitors from other provinces. Meat for a braai should always be of a good quality. Remember to grill marinated meats slowly to prevent scorching. For added flavour, baste the meat frequently with the marinade while braaiing. Always turn meat with a pair of tongs or an egg lifter to keep the juices sealed inside.

Menu

SNACKS AND MEATS:
Deep-fried mince parcels
Surprise parcels
Sliced bread rolls with samoosa filling
Tangy chicken drumsticks
Rice puffs
Braaied sosaties
Masala lamb chops
Grilled peri-peri snoek
Garlic bread

•

SALADS:
Pineapple and carrot salad
Bean and pepper salad
Pineapple and cabbage salad
Orange baskets

•

DESSERTS:
Ice-cream with apricot konfyt
Assorted fruit juices (see Beverages, page 76)

•

Peppermint coffee (page 77) and biscuits
(see Biscuits and Pastries, page 55)

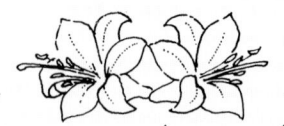

DEEP-FRIED MINCE PARCELS

These resemble Chinese spring rolls but are more spicy.

500 g lean minced beef or mutton
1 red pepper, finely chopped
1 green pepper, finely chopped
10 ml crushed garlic
1 green chilli, finely chopped
5 ml salt
2,5 ml white pepper
2,5 ml cayenne pepper
30 ml freshly squeezed lemon juice
500 g onions, finely chopped
30 ml cooking oil
15 ml chopped dhunia (coriander) leaves
5 ml freshly chopped mint leaves
1 kg frozen puff pastry (page 12)
oil for deep-frying

Fry minced beef, peppers, garlic, chilli, seasonings and lemon juice in a frying pan for about 10 minutes, stirring frequently to break up mince grains. Fry onions lightly in 30 ml oil, then add to meat mixture. Allow to cool before stirring in green dhunia leaves and mint. Defrost pastry and roll out into a rectangle, about 40 cm x 70 cm. Trim and cut into strips of 5 cm x 15 cm. Place a spoonful of meat mixture at one end of each strip and roll up tightly, pressing edges together to seal. Deep-fry in hot oil for 4–5 minutes until golden brown. Drain on paper towel.
MAKES ABOUT 36.

SURPRISE PARCELS

These savoury snacks consist of milk rolls filled with a curried mince filling and are very popular with children.

6 x 250 ml cake flour
200 ml self-raising flour
5 ml salt
20 ml sugar
100 g butter or margarine
1 x 10 g packet instant dried yeast
250 ml lukewarm milk
150 ml lukewarm water
1 egg, lightly beaten
30 ml milk for coating
curry mince filling (page 13)

Sift together flours and salt in a mixing bowl. Add sugar and rub in butter or margarine to make a crumbly mixture. Add instant dried yeast and stir. Combine milk and water and add to flour mixture. Knead until dough is fairly soft, adding more water if necessary. Moisten hands with oil and smooth over dough. Cover dough with plastic and leave to rise until doubled in bulk, about 1½–2 hours. Punch down and shape into balls. Make a hole in centre of each ball and fill with about 10 ml filling, sealing dough around filling very well. Place on greased baking sheet and leave to rise, about 30 minutes. Mix egg and 30 ml milk and coat tops of rolls. Bake at 180 °C for 20–25 minutes or until well risen and lightly golden on top. Serve warm or cold.
MAKES 24 ROLLS.

Cook's tip
Active dried yeast may also be used. Mix with 5 ml sugar and 150 ml lukewarm water and set aside for about 10 minutes, or until mixture starts to froth. Add to dry ingredients, then add milk and proceed as above.

SLICED BREAD ROLLS WITH SAMOOSA FILLING

A tasty way of using up leftover samoosa filling.

12 slices white bread (preferably 1 day old)
samoosa filling (page 12)
1 egg, lightly beaten

Remove crusts and roll bread with rolling pin. Place about 10 ml samoosa filling (page 12) of your choice on one end of each slice and roll up tightly. Roll each bread roll in waxed paper or clingwrap and refrigerate for 6 hours to allow bread to stick together. Remove covering and brush rolls with egg. Deep-fry until golden brown. Alternatively, bake in preheated oven at 200 °C for about 10 minutes or until golden brown.
MAKES 12 ROLLS.

TANGY CHICKEN DRUMSTICKS

30 ml soft butter
65 ml tomato chutney
15 ml soy sauce
10 ml Worcestershire sauce
10 ml tomato sauce
10 ml brown sugar
5 ml curry powder
2,5 ml chilli powder or cayenne pepper
750 g chicken drumsticks
lettuce leaves and green and red pepper rings for garnishing

Melt butter in a saucepan and stir in chutney, sauces, sugar, curry and chilli powder or cayenne pepper. Add chicken and coat well. Transfer chicken and sauce to a bowl and refrigerate, covered, for about 6 hours or overnight. Braai on coals, turning frequently to prevent burning. Serve on a bed of crisp lettuce and garnish with green and red pepper rings.
SERVES 6–8.

VARIATION
Cut off bottom end of drumsticks, reserving the meaty parts. Stir-fry chicken in 15 ml butter or oil until cooked through, about 30 minutes.

RICE PUFFS

This is not only a tasty snack, but also an ideal way of using up leftover rice.

500 ml cooked rice
cooking oil for deep-frying

Spread the rice on a tray to dry out completely, approximately 24 hours. Heat oil in a deep saucepan and fry dried-out rice until it puffs up. Remove rice from oil with a slotted spoon and drain on paper towel. Serve as a snack. Serves 4-6.

Cook's tip
Colour rice with food colouring before drying-out.

OUTDOOR ENTERTAINING

BRAAIED SOSATIES

For a sweet-and-sour variation, thread on dried apricots or peaches between cubes of meat.

1 x 1 kg leg of lamb, boned and cubed
200 g pickling onions, peeled and halved

MARINADE
5 bay leaves
5 ml fresh thyme sprigs (or 2,5 ml dried)
10 ml chopped fresh sage (or 5 ml dried)
15 ml curry powder
60 ml vinegar or lemon juice
50 ml sugar (or to taste)
10 ml crushed garlic
1 green chilli, finely chopped

Combine marinade ingredients and marinate meat and onions for at least 5 hours, preferably overnight. Thread cubed meat and onions onto sosatie skewers. Braai on grid for approximately 15 minutes, turning frequently to prevent burning.
SERVES 6.

Cook's tip
Soak wooden skewers in cold water for about 30 minutes prior to use to prevent them from burning.

MASALA LAMB CHOPS

These chops burn easily because of the sweet marinade, so it is advisable to grill over low heat.

1 kg lamb loin chops

MARINADE
10 ml crushed garlic
10 ml grated fresh root ginger
10 ml ground koljander (coriander)
30 ml cooking oil
30 ml fruit or tomato chutney
5 ml salt
5 ml crushed, dried red chillies
30 ml lemon juice
10 ml paprika

Combine all ingredients and coat both sides of the chops. Leave to stand for 2–4 hours. Braai meat on grid for about 15 minutes, turning frequently to prevent burning.
SERVES 6.

VARIATION
Shallow-fry marinated chops in 30 ml heated oil in a frying pan until well browned on both sides, approximately 10 minutes a side.

GRILLED PERI-PERI SNOEK

1 whole snoek, gutted and cleaned

MARINADE
25 ml crushed garlic
10 ml peri-peri powder
10 ml paprika
10 ml salt
45 ml freshly squeezed lemon juice
50 ml melted butter

Halve snoek and cut into large portions. Wash, drain and pat dry with paper towel. Combine marinade ingredients and brush over fleshy side of snoek. Place on braai grid, fleshy side down, and braai for about 5–8 minutes, making sure that fish is not too close to fire. Turn fish and braai for another 5 minutes or until fish is golden brown, brushing frequently with marinade. Serve hot with lemon wedges.
SERVES 12.

GARLIC BREAD

1 long French loaf
15 ml crushed garlic
60 ml soft butter
5 ml dried mixed herbs

Preheat oven to 180 °C. Without cutting through base, cut French loaf into slices about 2 cm wide. Mix garlic, butter and mixed herbs together and spread on both sides of each slice. Wrap bread in foil and bake in preheated oven for about 20 minutes. Open foil, increase oven temperature to 220 °C and bake until crispy, 5–10 minutes. Serve hot.
SERVES 10.

PINEAPPLE AND CARROT SALAD

1 large pineapple, peeled and grated
7 large carrots, finely grated
5 ml sugar (optional)
5 ml crushed, dried red chillies (optional)

Mix all ingredients together. Serve in a glass bowl lined with crisp lettuce leaves.
SERVES 10.

BEAN AND PEPPER SALAD

1 x 410 g can baked beans
1 small onion, finely sliced
1 small green pepper, diced
15 ml white or brown vinegar
10 ml sugar
5 ml crushed, dried red chillies

Combine all ingredients in a saucepan and heat to boiling point, stirring frequently. Serve hot or cold.
SERVES 8.

PINEAPPLE AND CABBAGE SALAD

1 pineapple, grated
1 apple, peeled and grated
½ small cabbage, finely shredded
5 radishes, grated
45 ml mayonnaise
15 ml tomato sauce
2,5 ml freshly ground black pepper
salt to taste

In a large bowl, combine pineapple, apple, cabbage and radishes. Mix together mayonnaise, tomato sauce, black pepper and salt. Combine with rest of ingredients and stir to blend well.
SERVES 10.

ORANGE BASKETS

These festive baskets can also be served as a starter to a spicy meal.

80 ml sultanas
2 small green apples, peeled and cored
juice of 1 lemon
6 oranges
500 g carrots, peeled and finely grated
2 sticks table celery, finely chopped
25 ml sugar
5 ml garlic steak seasoning
30 ml chopped dhunia (coriander) leaves (optional)
30 ml chopped pistachio nuts for garnishing

Soak sultanas in boiling water for 15 minutes, then drain. Grate apples coarsely and sprinkle with lemon juice to prevent discolouring. Halve 4 oranges, cutting into a zigzag shape for a more decorative effect. Scoop out flesh, reserving shells. Chop flesh into small chunks, discarding white pith and pips. Peel remaining oranges and finely chop flesh, discarding white pith and pips. Mix together sultanas, apples, orange flesh, carrots, celery, sugar, garlic steak seasoning and dhunia leaves. Set aside for 20 minutes. Fill orange shells with salad and sprinkle pistachio nuts over to garnish.
MAKES 8.

ICE-CREAM WITH APRICOT KONFYT

An unusual but delicious way of eating konfyt. It is usually served on its own or as a sweet at weddings and feasts.

3 x 250 g packets dried apricots
500 ml water
500 ml sugar
3 whole cloves
2 pieces stick cinnamon

Soak apricots in water for 1 hour, then transfer (with water) to a heavy-based saucepan. Sprinkle sugar over and add spices. Cook over low heat for 1 hour, stirring occasionally. Apricots must be tender and syrup thick. Serve with vanilla ice-cream.
SERVES 10.

Index

Atjars
- carrot and apple 45
- green chilli, stuffed 45
- lemon, easy 45

Barakat
- engagement 5
- ghajad 5

Beverages
- almond milk 77
- fruit juice, fresh 76
- ginger beer punch, Zoe's fizzy 76
- mango juice 76
- orange juice, spicy 77
- peppermint coffee 77
- rose syrup 77
- spanspek shake 76
- tropical fruit punch 77

Biscuits
- afghan 57
- cherry nut balls 61
- chocolate chip cookies 56
- chocolate drops 56
- coconut and almond scraps 57
- coconut nests 60
- custard biscuits (variation) 60
- date and coconut 56
- gingernut scraps 55
- granadilla 60
- honey and coconut 60
- melting moments 56
- melt-in-the-mouths 61
- pecan nut scraps 57
- peppermint fingers 55
- shortbread fingers 60
- shortbread surprises 57
- spitz cookies (variation) 73

Bread
- banana loaf, flop-proof 49
- basket 84
- breakfast cakes 53
- buns, soft milk 53
- buns, spicy fruit 52
- doughnuts, quick ring 48
- garlic 94
- lemon fruit plait 48
- muffins, bran 53
- pineapple tea 52
- pumpkin bollas 52
- rotis, Malay 47
- scones, buttermilk 52
- savoury cheese loaf 49
- wholewheat, instant 49
- wholewheat loaf 49

Bride's dinner basket 82

Cake
- apple 69
- banana and walnut loaf 69
- carrot loaf, boiled 69
- cheesecake, marshmallow 68
- cherry and sultana loaf 69
- chocolate marble 68
- chocolate orange 68
- coconut, golden 65
- coconut, moist 66
- fruit-layered 64
- fruit, light 64
- granadilla 64
- lemon butter 66
- orange, tangy 63
- pineapple coconut 65
- pineapple, upside-down 65
- sponge, caramel 66
- sponge, caramel and cream 65
- sponge flans 66
- Swiss roll, vanilla cream 63

Cakes (small)
- apple tartlets 74
- butterfly 73
- chocolate cream puffs 73
- custard tartlets 74
- fruit tartlets 74
- tri-colour snowballs 73

Catering for large numbers 88

Chicken
- akhni 27
- breasts, crumbed 26
- breyani 29
- chilli 17
- curry, tomato 28
- drumsticks, tangy 93
- kebabs 30
- pot-roast, paprika 28
- salad, spicy 28
- soup, giblet 27
- spicy yoghurt 28
- stir-fried 30
- tandoori 28
- tikka 30
- with prunes, masala 28

Dessert
- apple meringue delight 70
- apple cream pie 70
- banana, custard and cream delight 72
- gestoofde droë vrugte 85
- ice-cream with apricot konfyt 95
- lemon meringue coconut slices 72
- potato pudding 85
- rainbow jelly 85
- strawberry pudding 85
- tropical fruit tart 72
- trifle, fruit 81
- trifle, tropical fruit 72
- vanilla squares with granadilla 70

Doopmaal 5

Eid celebration dinner 5, 79

Fillings for gevulde nessies 16
- chicken liver 16
- prawn 16
- sheep brain 16

Fillings for samoosas 12
- chicken 12
- fish 12
- mince 12
- mixed vegetable 12
- potato 12

Fillings for savoury pies 13
- chicken and mushroom 13
- curry mince 13
- steak and kidney 13

Fish
- curry (variation) 21
- dry spicy masala 24
- frikkadels 24
- skate wings, smoored 25
- snoek, grilled (variation) 19
- snoek, grilled peri-peri 94
- snoek roe, fried 25
- snoek roe, smoored (variation) 25
- stokvis bobotie 25

Funerals 5

Herbs 7-9

Meat
- bobotie (steak mince) 82
- bredie, tomato frikkadel 33
- breyani, mutton 80, 88
- curry, lamb and tomato 32
- curry, mutton 83, 88
- curry, mutton and lentil 36
- curry with brinjals, mince 33
- curry with gem squash, gheema 37
- denningvleis 83
- frikkadels, oven 37
- frikkadels with tomato and spaghetti 36
- kebabs, liver 37
- kebabs, seekh 37
- kebabs with chutney dip 17
- kidneys, fried 38
- Malaysian-style beef 33
- masala lamb chops 94
- mavrou 88
- mince pilau, gheema 36
- mince parcels, deep-fried 92
- ox tongue, boiled 38
- ox tongue, garlic roast 38
- pootjies en boonjies 38
- pot-roast leg of lamb 79
- pot-roast masala leg chops 33
- sosatie chops 83
- sosaties, braaied 94
- stew, mutton and vegetable 32

Outdoor entertainment 92

Paaper 11

Pastry(ies)
- fancy puff 61
- horns 61
- puff 12
- pur 11

Pizza, quick-and-easy 48
Puris, Indian 84

Ramadan 5, 79

Rice
- almond yellow 81
- gesmoorde ertjie rys 44
- gesmoorde rys 91
- puffs 93

Rotis, Malay 47

Salad
- bean and pepper 95
- beetroot and onion 81
- mixed fruit and vegetable 84
- orange baskets 95
- pineapple and cabbage 95
- pineapple and carrot 95
- spicy chicken 28
- tomato and onion 84

Salomi 47

Sambals
- apple, quince and pineapple 44
- cucumber 91
- cucumber and pineapple 45
- cucumber, onion and celery 45
- tomato and onion 91

Seafood (see also Fish)
- akhni 21
- calamari rings, deep-fried 25
- crayfish breyani 20
- crayfish cocktail 19
- crayfish curry (variation) 21
- crayfish tails, grilled 19
- perlemoen curry, minced 24
- perlemoen frikkadels 24
- prawn breyani (variation) 20
- prawn curry 21
- prawn cutlets 21
- prawns, Malaysian 20
- prawns, stir-fried 20

Seasonings 7-9

Snacks
- bhajias (variation) 17
- bread cups 16
- chilli bites (see dhaltjies)
- chilli chicken (variation) 17
- chilli kingklip (variation) 17
- dhaltjies 17
- dhaltjies, sweetcorn (variation) 17
- gevulde nessies (see also Fillings) 16
- kebabs with chutney dip 17
- polony wrappers 16
- rice puffs 93
- samoosas (see also Fillings) 11
- sausage ropes 17
- savoury pies (see also Fillings) 12
- sliced bread rolls with samoosa filling 93
- spicy roasted nuts 17

Soup
- chicken giblet 27
- vegetable (variation) 27

Spices 7-9

Vegetables
- baby marrow curry (variation) 41
- brinjals with garlic, braised 41
- cauliflower curry 41
- dhal sauce with braised onion 44
- carrot and potato curry, dry 41
- carrots, glazed baby 80
- corn, dry spicy 42
- ertjie rys, gesmoorde 44
- fritters 42
- gem squash, stuffed 80
- okra curry 41
- potato and pea curry 40
- potato curry, dry spicy 40
- potatoes, crispy 81
- potatoes, mashed 83
- stir-fry, Malaysian 42
- sweetcorn lagan 42
- turnips, braised 44

Weddings 5